THE DIGO MISSION OF THE ANGLICAN CHURCH OF KENYA:

ESSAYS IN COMMEMORATION OF
114 YEARS OF MISSION WORK IN
KWALE COUNTRY (1904-2018)

Compiling Editor
Julius Mutugi Gathogo

English Language Editor
Sarah Wallace

First Fruits Press
Wilmore, Kentucky
c2020

ISBN: 9781621719984

The Digo Mission: Essays in Commemoration of 114 Years of Mission Work in East Africa (1904-2018)
Compiling editor, Julius Mutugi Gathogo
English language editor, Sarah Wallace
First Fruits Press, ©2020
Digital version at https://place.asburyseminary.edu/academicbooks/34

First Fruits Press is a digital imprint of the Asbury Theological Seminary, B.L. Fisher Library. Asbury Theological Seminary is the legal owner of the material previously published by the Pentecostal Publishing Co. and reserves the right to release new editions of this material as well as new material produced by Asbury Theological Seminary. Its publications are available for noncommercial and educational uses, such as research, teaching and private study. First Fruits Press has licensed the digital version of this work under the Creative Commons Attribution Noncommercial 3.0 United States License. To view a copy of this license, visit http://creativecommons.org/licenses/by-nc/3.0/us/.

For all other uses, contact:
First Fruits Press
B.L. Fisher Library
Asbury Theological Seminary
204 N. Lexington Ave.
Wilmore, KY 40390
http://place.asburyseminary.edu/firstfruits

The Digo mission: essays in commemoration of 114 years of mission work in East Africa (1904-2018)
    The Digo mission: essays in commemoration of 114 years of mission work in East Africa (1904-2018) / compiling editor, Julius Mutugi Gathogo ; English language editor, Sarah Wallace. Wilmore, Kentucky : First Fruits Press, ©2020.
    ISBN: 9781621719984 (paperback)
    ISBN: 9780914368069 (uPDF)
    ISBN: 9780914368076 (Mobi)
    OCLC: 1117709853
    1. Missions--Kenya. 2. Kenya--Church history. 3. Kwale County (Kenya)--Church history. 4. Anglican Church of Kenya--Missions--History. 5. Digo (African people)--Religion.
    I. Gathogo, Julius Mutugi. II. Wallace, Sarah.
BX5700.55.A44 D53 2020

Cover design by April Hardman

asburyseminary.edu
800.2ASBURY
204 North Lexington Avenue
Wilmore, Kentucky 40390

First Fruits Press
The Academic Open Press of Asbury Theological Seminary
204 N. Lexington Ave., Wilmore, KY 40390
859-858-2236
first.fruits@asburyseminary.edu
asbury.to/firstfruits

TABLE OF CONTENTS

Dedication	i
Foreword	v
Acknowledgements	xi
Preface	xiii
Contributors	xvii
Abbreviations & Acronyms	xix
Timeline of Kwale Church History	xxi
Important Anglican Church Leaders in Kenya's History	xxiii
Kwale County Map	xxv

Chapter 1: Itineration in the Digo Country: July 16-28, 1912
    Geo. W. Wright 1

Chapter 2: Culture, Identity and Power in the Digo Mission
    Ferdinand Manjewa M'bwangi . . . 11

Chapter 3: First European Missionaries in Digo land
    Bryson K. Samboja 25

Chapter 4: Pioneer Digo-Duruma Christian Converts
    Japheth Muthoka 33

Chapter 5. Christianity in Viongwani, Kwale Country
    Robert Maneno 41

Chapter 6: Anglican Church in Kwale Country: A Brief History
    Peter Mwangi 53

Chapter 7: Christian-Muslim Relations in Digo Land: A Historical Perspective
    Evans Mwangi 61

Chapter 8: Unsung Heroes and Heroines in the Digo Mission
    Julius Gathogo 71

Chapter 9: Womens' Participation in the Digo mission
    Lawrence Tsawe-Munga Chidongo . . . 89

Chapter 10: Protestants and Pentecostal Churches: A Survey
    Joshua Itumo Kiilu 99

Chapter 11: Challenges and Prospects in the Digo Mission
    Julius Gathogo 109

Chapter 12: Global Team Mission in Digo Land
    Josephat J. Murutu 125

Chapter 13: Conclusion: What Can World Christianity Learn From Kwale County?
    Robert A. Danielson 137

Works Cited 147

DEDICATION

To the men and women who have gallantly worked hard to promote the elusive Digo Mission and to Bishop Alphonce Mwaro Baya who commissioned this research on 114 years of the Digo mission (1904-2018) in Kenya.

Members of Diocesan Research Unit (DRU) with the focus group for Digo Mission:

L to R: F. Manjewa, B.K. Samboja, J. Mwalonya, Mzee Mumbo Munga, T.M. Chidongo, P. Mwangi, J. Mwayadi, J.M. Gathogo, J.I. Kiilu, E.B. Ramtu, E. Mwangi, S. Maneno and J. Muthoka.

L to R: J. J. Maneno, Elijjak K. Zani, Stephen Zani, Mchungaji S. Pore Maneno, Rev. Makame.

FOREWORD

I am delighted to write this foreword for the project that I commissioned in September 2018; a fine book that is entitled: *The Digo Mission of the Anglican Church of Kenya: Essays in Commemoration of 114 Years of Mission Work in Kwale Country (1904-2018)*. From the outset, let me confess that this is a Mombasa Diocesan achievement, a regional achievement, and indeed a legacy that will hopefully stand the test of time. Some of the key issues that appear in this book include: identity and culture in the Digo mission, the first Digo-Duruma converts to Christianity, the first European missionaries in Digo land, women's participation in the Digo mission, Christian-Muslim relations in the Digo mission, Gospel and culture in the Digo mission, challenges in the Digo mission, and the future of Christian missions. Considering that the written word will always earn its infinity, in one way or the other, this publication ensures that our legacy will never be swept under the carpet.

The publication will thus speak to the present and to the future generations. It will inspire researchers in the Digo mission and the rest of the East African coast. With this publication, more post-graduate researchers will now rediscover that there is something good from Digo land. In light of this, I am reminded about John 1:45-46 where Philp found Nathaniel and told him, "We have found the One Moses wrote about in the Law, the One the prophets foretold – Jesus of Nazareth, the son of Joseph." Nathaniel then asked: "Can anything good come from Nazareth?" Philip answered: "Come and see!" In planning, researching, and subsequently publishing this piece of art, we all have become little Philips telling doubting Thomases, "Come and see!" As a historical document, it will help the future generations avoid the mistakes of the past. It will also help us, the policy makers and the ordinary Christians, to understand ourselves better; and indeed appreciate the intrigues surrounding our mission today. In understanding where we are coming from, we find a gateway to understanding where we are going as a people of God.

The Digo mission is the most interesting of the many missions that are a result of the 19th and 20th century European missionary activities that began in 1844 after the arrival of Rev. Dr. Johann Ludwig Krapf. Since then, several missions came up and went on to surpass the Digo mission which is 40 kilometres away from the Kisauni-Freretown mission that was established in 1875. Other missions across East Africa, and which was once the Diocese of Eastern Equatorial Africa (1884-1897), and later the Mombasa Diocese (since 1897) are: the Baganda mission of 1876-77, the Moshi mission of 1878, the Sagalla mission (1883), the Jilore mission (1890), the Mbale mission (1900), the Kabete mission (1900), the Weithaga mission (1904), the Kaloleni mission (1904), the Wusi mission (1905), the Kahuhia mission (1906), Nairobi (1906), the Maseno (1906), Kisumu (1909), the Kabare mission of 1910, Kigari (1910), Mutira (1912), Butere (1912), the Rwanda mission of 1916-19, the Ng'iya mission of 1921, the Kacheliba mission of 1929, the Marsabit mission of 1930, and the Burundi mission of 1934, among others.

While the Digo mission of 1904 began much earlier than others such as the Maseno mission of 1906, the Rwanda mission of 1916, the Marsabit mission of 1930, and the Butere mission of 1912, the former remains an underdog with little to boast of 114 years later. In some of the above missions such as the Maseno (1906) and the Kabete (1900) missions, their other respective numerical strength, their human resources and their diverse resources have enabled them to grow from one level to another; and eventually to graduate into countless parishes, deaneries, and archdeaconries plus over a dozen dioceses. What went wrong in the Digo mission of 1904? Even if we had two archdeaconries by 2018, two deaneries and about 15 parishes, we have yet to reach our target. What is the problem with our evangelism that leaves the fate of 20% of present day Kwale County (Digo land) as adherents of traditional African religion when the Gospel of Christ came to illumine the world of the Digo and Duruma peoples? What about in the rest of the world? As the writer of Hebrews (2:3) passionately says, "How shall we escape if we neglect so great a salvation, which was first announced by the Lord, and was confirmed to us by those who heard Him; and was affirmed by God through signs, wonders, various miracles, and gifts of the Holy Spirit distributed according to His will?" How can over 90% of Kwale County (Digo land) escape this great salvation?

With the percentage of Christians in Kwale County, the center of the Digo mission, falling below 3% of the population, 114 years after it was begun, we are bound to undertake a review of our operations. This ultimately drives us to ask: Have we failed to employ the various Christological and Pauline methods in mission? Have we failed this interesting strategy in mission where St Paul in 1 Corinthians 9:22 says, "To the weak, I became weak, to win the weak. I have become all things to all people so that by all possible means I might save some"? This method of reaching peoples in their diverse situations, cultures, contexts, and ironically employing their own methods, can be used to counter the anti-Christ in the Digo mission. Similarly, Christ's incarnational model of mission shows the level to which we can go in our bid to win and save some. In the nature of things, we must highlight Christ's incarnational model that is well captured by St. Paul (Phil 2:6-7) when he says:

> ...who, existing in the form of God, did not consider equality with God something to be grasped, but emptied Himself, taking the form of a servant, being made in human likeness. And being found in appearance as a man, He humbled Himself and became obedient to death—even death on a cross....

Remember, Jesus Christ did not say, "Go and save souls" (the salvation of souls is the supernatural work of God), but He said, "Go... make disciples of all the nations...." Yet you cannot make disciples unless you are a disciple yourself. When the disciples returned from their first mission, they were filled with joy because even the demons were subject to them. But Jesus said, in effect, "Don't rejoice in successful service—the great secret of joy is that you have the right relationship with Me" (Luke 10:17-20). The missionary's great essential is remaining true to the call of God, and realizing that his or her one and only purpose is to disciple men and women to Jesus.

Considering that the mission is an activity of the people of faith, we must redefine, reassess, and rethink the strategies in the Digo mission afresh; and eventually establish whether the old approaches of Henry Venn's (1796-1873) Three-Selfs (self-propagation by locals or indigenous people, self-sustaining by relying on local resources only, and self-governing) will do. But even then, I am confident that we have met most of its expectations and still have to do more. Like St. Paul, we might need to view our mission in Digo land in terms of 'movement' (Paul sent to the Gentiles) and in terms of 'intentionality' (to proclaim Christ and his resurrection) as in Galatians 1:1, 15:15. If we think of ourselves as modern missionaries, then we must pose and ask ourselves the hard questions that will eventually trigger the answer for a myriad of concerns in the Digo mission:

- First: who is a modern missionary – a 21st century missionary?
- Second: do we have anything to learn from the previous missionaries?
- Third: how did the apostolic missionaries conduct their discourses?
- Fourth: can we learn anything from St Paul's missionary goals such as: reaching as many people as possible, establishing new churches, communities of followers of Christ – Jews and Gentiles, men and women, free and slave – and engaging in a teaching ministry so that believers are equipped among other goals? (Col. 1:25-29)
- Fifth: St. Paul was the leading theologian in the Mediterranean region whose goals and strategies were heavily relied upon by the general populace. We too can grow to the 'maturity' of St Paul and be relied upon to offer a theo-social direction as the need arises, to our respective peoples.

Having said this, I must hasten to thank the members of the Diocesan Research Unit (DRU) of Mombasa Diocese who have been meeting to strategize on the Digo mission in both Kwale and Mombasa Counties - all in their bid to serve via the media of publication, since September 2018. Working on a book publication or for a periodical in two-month's time is not a mean achievement. The team has burnt its midnight oil so as to help in rejuvenating the Digo mission through well-researched documentation. They Include: Rev. Dr. Ferdinand Manjewa M'bwangi (Chair), Rev. Dr. Julius Gathogo, Ven. Dr. Bryson K. Samboja Treasurer), Rev. Evans Mwangi (Secretary), Rev. Dr. Tsawe-Chidongo, Ven. Canon. Dr Dorcas Kiundu, Rev. Josphat Murutu, Rev. Mary Michere Kiundu, the Very Rev. Festus Kiseu, the Rev. Gerald Ngumbao and, Dr. Robert J. Maneno. As their activities on the Digo mission gained momentum, more were invited from the Kwale Team. That included: Dr. Japheth Muthoka, Rev. Peter Mwangi, Ven. Elijah Ramtu, and Rev. Joshua Kiilu. In using their own resources, the DRU team have researched and eventually prepared a credible book that will help us in making policies regarding the Digo mission now, and in the future. Their credible work will open up research on the Digo mission locally and abroad as the huge gaping holes cited in their research calls for further research. With this starting point, the wonderful exploratory journey has begun. I commend this publication to researchers, the practitioners of the Christian faith and all policy makers in this region. As we read the contents herein, we shall be encouraged to do more, and indeed plan better. Welcome!

Rt. Rev. Alphonce Mwaro Baya, BTH, MTH, MPHIL
Bishop of Mombasa

ACKNOWLEDGEMENTS

We wish to thank the Anglican Bishop of Mombasa, Rt. Rev. Alphonce Mwaro Baya, for commissioning the research on 114 years of the Digo mission. In forming the Diocesan Research Unit (DRU) and subsequently assigning it the research on the Digo mission, Bishop Baya has demonstrated his love and concern for Digo land and the general society that makes the Diocese of Mombasa.

We wish to thank all the members of the Diocesan Research Unit (DRU): Rev. Dr. Ferdinand Manjewa M'bwangi (Chair), Rev. Dr. Julius Gathogo (Vice- Chair), Ven. Dr. Bryson Samboja (Treasurer), Rev. Evans Mwangi (Secretary), Rev. Dr. Lawrence ('Munga' deleted) Tsawe-Munga Chidongo, Ven. Canon Dr. Dorcas Kiundu, Rev. Gerald Ngumbao, Rev. Josphat Murutu, Rev. Michelle Kiundu and, Dr. Robert J. Maneno, for their ability to speed up the assignment that was done in a few months. Their ability to come up with brilliant ideas within a short time is inspirational – as it shows that African woes are surmountable in all spheres of life. In other words, they chose to work rather than merely to spectate, as others build their walls (Nehemiah 2:18). Hence, they "started building" till the wall was completed.

Another group that deserves our mention is the Kwale Team that was planning centenary celebrations for the Digo mission. It included: Rev Peter Mwangi, Rev. Joshua Itumo Kiilu (a Pentecostal church leader), and Dr. Japheth Muthoka. Like the *am hareetz* (those who did not go to exile during the Babylonian conquest), they did not allow for exclusion from this all-important project of reconstructing the Digo mission. Some have papers that appear in this book. They were also able to beat the deadlines, just as the Mombasa Team. In merging both the Mombasa

Team and the Kwale Team, unveiling the Digo mission became not only a lively project but also a do-able job.

Equally deserving our compliments are the Digo elders who met the Mombasa team at an old Golden Guest House on the 9th and 10th of October 2018 and willingly provided much needed information about the Digo mission. Led by the retired Ven. Canon Elijah Kubeta Mwahuruma Ramtu, the elders were very resourceful. Others included: David Dawa, Samuel Maneno, Juma Mwayadi, Munga Mumbo, Shadrack Mwalonya, and Rev. Simeon Pore Maneno among others.

To our publishers and others whose names remain unnoticed, we salute you too! You are the true heroes and heroines of the Digo mission. We thank you for your small contributions here and there.

PREFACE

In their first meeting at Diocesan Board Room, Mombasa, on Tuesday September 25, 2018, the Diocesan Research Unit (DRU) agreed with Bishop Alphonce Baya's proposal on the idea of documenting the history of the Digo mission (1904-2018). In their reasoning, a credible document on the Digo mission will not only guide future research, but will also help policy makers in understanding the matters at hand. In other words, a credible research on the Digo mission would set the pace on our mission histories locally and beyond our region. In understanding where the Digo mission is coming from, it is possible to reassess its mission for the future.

In the Mombasa Board Room meeting of September 2018, several issues and methods were discussed in regard to strategies of researching the Digo mission. First, it was appreciated that the Digo mission refers to the present Kwale County. This is an area that is occupied by the predominantly Digo sub-group of the larger Mijikenda community. It is also occupied by another Mijikenda sub-group, the Duruma. The Kamba community also has a sizeable presence, just as other migrants. Nevertheless, the presence of the Muslim community, which makes up over 75% of the population, is a noticeable feature.

In our interviews, we could hear strange stories about the beliefs in witchcraft among the locals. We would also hear about the girl who was buried alive at Chinondo, past Ukunda, between Msambweni and Mwabungo – all in the anti-Christ's bid to stop the establishment of Christianity in Digo land. We also heard about the death and burial of Mrs. Elizabeth Bans and her daughter due to heavy bouts of Malaria. Malaria, as a tropical disease, has had its casualties in the Digo mission and in the larger East African mission. Elizabeth Bans was the wife of the first resident Church Missionary Society clergy to Digo land, Rev. Bans.

In view of the foregoing, this book seeks to locate the Digo mission 114 years later (1904-2018). In other words, how has the Digo mission progressed since 1904 when Rev. Bans set a centre at Zunguni, started a school, church, and constructed more churches? The concern for over a hundred years of Christian missions in Digo land prompted us to ask ourselves several questions:

- How can we address the identity and cultures of the Digo people?
- Who were the first missionaries in Digo land?
- Who were the first Digo/Duruma converts in the history of the mission?
- Who were the first Anglican missionaries in Digo land?
- How does the Christian-Muslim relationship in Digo land manifest itself?
- Who are the unsung heroes and heroines in the Digo mission?
- Are there clear roles for women in the Digo mission since its inception?
- How do Pentecostals, Independents and other churches fare in the Digo mission?
- What are the challenges and prospects for the Digo mission?
- And what is the future of Christianity in Digo land?

While the last question can be answered easily by considering that there are heightened activities in the Digo mission, which appear to guarantee the future of the Digo mission, the challenge of leadership remains another critical issue. Will the ministers in the Digo mission offer transformative leadership that empowers everyone to take responsibility? Do the ministers in the Digo mission offer transactional leadership that just seeks to maintain the status quo? Will the leadership in the Digo mission appreciate that it is not enough to be a servant leader; and that a transformative leader does better?

The above questions, which came up as the members of the DRU were navigating through the methods of documenting the history of the Digo mission, informs the nature of the chapters in this book. The book, as in the case of Genesis 1 and 2, allows the various accounts to speak for themselves. This has sadly allowed some limited repetitions as some issues had to be repeated in order to allow each presenter to make his or her case from an informed position. While the contents are in harmony, without undue repetitions, the individual researcher was allowed to table and publish his or her findings. The book follows the new 21st century skills movement in education – a phenomenon where education is geared towards solving the myriad problems facing diverse societies. The new skills also includes technology-driven education, a phenomenon that the DRU often exploited as they emailed respondents, called via cell phones, employed both fieldwork and desk-top research; and used other forms of technology to document the mission histories. The 21st century skills movement in education also includes collaborative and joint research, joint publications, and joint revision of syllabi and curriculum. In brainstorming on these matters before and after we went to do joint research, we were able to become good stewards of our time.

In reading this book, we hope it will be of benefit to everyone who has an interest in mission historiographies and African missions since the 19th century. In considering that the written word lives longer than the writer; we hope this book will be preserved well in our libraries, churches, schools, and on our individual bookshelves. It will help mission strategists to understand mission challenges and prospects; and eventually guide the future in identifying the way forward in the mission. Certainly, those who ignore history are bound to repeat the mistakes of the past. May God help us to learn from the history of the Digo mission.

CONTRIBUTORS

1. Ferdinand Manjewa M'bwangi (PhD) graduated in July 2019 with a PhD (Religious studies) from the University of Cape Town, South Africa. He is a fulltime lecturer in the Department of Philosophy & Religious Studies at Pwani University (Kilifi, Kenya), a Post-Doctoral Research Fellow at the University of Pretoria (South Africa) and, an ordained Priest in the Anglican Diocese of Mombasa. He has a number of publications in refereed journals.

2. Julius Gathogo, PhD, is a Senior Lecturer, Department of Philosophy and Religious Studies, School of Humanities and Social Sciences, Kenyatta University, Mombasa Campus. He has researched extensively locally and abroad. He has over 100 publications as book chapters, refereed journals, and individually authored books. He is the author of *Beyond Mount Kenya Region* (2017).

3. Lawrence Tsawe-Munga Chidongo, PhD, is a lecturer at Pwani University, Department of Philosophy and Religious Studies, School of Humanities and Social Sciences. He has several publications on religio-cultural concerns. He is also a Methodist Minister from Kwale County.

4. Japheth Muthoka is a veterinary doctor serving in Digo land, an Anglican lay leader, and a community mobilizer.

5. Joshua Itumo Kiilu is a Pentecostal pastor, ministering in Digo land.

6. Peter Mwangi is a member of the ordained Anglican clergy, an Area Dean, ministering in Kwale County, at the heart of Digo land.

7. Bryson K. Samboja (Dmiss.) is a member of the ordained clergy in the Anglican Church of Kenya. He has served in the diocese in Kenya since 1984, nine years of which he served as the principal of Bishop Hannington Institute, preparing ordinands for full-time ministry, and now is the director of Global Team missions in Kwale and Africa, at large.

8. Rev. Josephat J. Murutu is a member of the ordained clergy in the Anglican Diocese of Mombasa with a wealth of experience in pastoral ministry.

9. Rev. Evans Mwangi is a member of the ordained clergy in the Anglican Diocese of Mombasa who is actively involved in the implementation of Bishop Alphonce Mwaro's four-pillar diocesan strategic plan.

10. Robert Maneno, PhD, hails from Vyongwani, Kwale County. He is a full time lecturer at Pwani University and active lay communicant in the Anglican diocese of Mombasa.

11. Sarah Wallace hails from Kinango, Kwale County. She is the English language editor of this monograph and a full time lecturer in French at Pwani University.

12. Robert Danielson, PhD, is a missiologist and Scholarly Communications Librarian at Asbury Theological Seminary in Wilmore, Kentucky in the United States. He has edited this volume for publication and added the first chapter from research into missions in Digo land by Rev. George Wright. He has also written a conclusion chapter for this volume.

ABBREVIATIONS & ACRONYMS

ACK:	Anglican Church of Kenya
AIR:	African Indigenous Religions
BTH:	Bachelor of Theology
BTL:	Bible Translation and Literature
CE:	Common Era
CMS:	Church Missionary Society
ECDE:	Early Childhood Development Education
KEWASNET:	Kenya Water Agriculture and Sanitation Network
MHURI:	Muslim for Human Rights
MTH:	Master of Theology
NGOs:	Non-Governmental Organizations
TSC:	Teachers Service Commission
Ven:	Venerable
FDG:	Fows Discussion Group

TIMELINE OF KWALE CHURCH HISTORY

12th Century (or before)- Islam arrives in Mombasa

1498- Portuguese Vasco da Gama arrives in Mombasa

1500- Portuguese sacked Mombasa

1528- Portuguese attacked Mombasa again

1567- Augustinians set up Catholic Mission in Mombasa

1585- Emir 'Ali Bey and Muslim forces expel the Portuguese

1589- Portuguese retake Mombasa

1607- Catholic Brethren of Mercy arrive in Mombasa

1698- Portuguese expelled and Mombasa came under rule of Oman

1844- Johann Ludwig Krapf of CMS became the first Anglican missionary

1846- Johannes Rebmann of CMS arrived

1848- First Anglican church in Freretown

1862- Thomas Wakefield, first Methodist missionary arrived

1875- Mission focus on settlement of free slaves in Kisauni-Freretown

1882- Harry Kerr Binns arrives in Mombasa

1887- Mombasa relinquished to British East Africa Association

1891- Bible published in Swahili

1895- Mombasa under British administration

1902-1904- Roman Catholic Holy Ghost Fathers set up mission in Waa

1904-1912- Rev. Bans reported as CMS missionary in Zunguni

1913- Zunguni mission buildings reportedly burned in accidental fire by caretaker, Mwangauchi

1914- George Wright planted churches in Kwale County for CMS

1914-1918- World War I led to most churches failing except for Vyongwani.

1923- Waa Catholic School founded

1957- T. L. Osborn Healing Crusade in Mombasa

1958- Billy Graham Crusade in Kenya

1968- Oral Roberts Crusade in Kenya

1970- African Inland Church reaches Kwale by immigration with Samuel Nganda in Makobe

1971- African Brotherhood Church reaches Shimba Hills with M. Mawess

1975- Ven. Canon Elijah Kubeta Mwahuruma Ramtu becomes the first ordained Anglican Digo priest.

1970's- Kenya Assemblies of God spread to Kwale County.

Rev. Nimrod Mboje from Taita becomes the first clergyman working with Anglican churches in Kwale County.

1985- Rev. Simeon Pore Maneno becomes the second ordained Anglican Digo priest.

1980's- Baptists, Malcolm Heartnail, Richard Mang, and Wayne Richards of the African Inland Church arrive.

1990's- Ven. Dr. Bryson Samboja introduces work of Global Teams-Africa, Kenya to Kwale County.

2005- New Testament translated into the Digo language, Chidigo.

IMPORTANT ANGLICAN CHURCH LEADERS IN KENYA'S HISTORY

Vincent W. Ryan (1862-1872), Presiding Bishop of the Diocese of the Eastern Equatorial

James Hannington (1884-1885), Bishop of Eastern Equatorial Africa

Henry Perrot Parker (1886-1888, Bishop of Eastern Equatorial Africa

Alfred Robert Tucker (1890-1897), Bishop of Eastern Equatorial Africa

William George Peel (1897-1916), Bishop of Mombasa

Richard Stanley Heywood (1918-1936), Bishop of Mombasa

Reginald Percy Crabbe (1936-1953), Bishop of Mombasa

Leonard Beecher (1953-1960), Bishop of Mombasa

Leonard Beecher (1960-1970), Archbishop of East Africa

Peter Mwang'ombe (1964-1979), Bishop of Mombasa

Crispus Dolton Nzano (1980-1993), Bishop of Mombasa

Julius Robert Katoi Kalu (1994-2017), Bishop of Mombasa

Alphonce Mwaro Baya (2018-), Bishop of Mombasa

KWALE COUNTY MAP

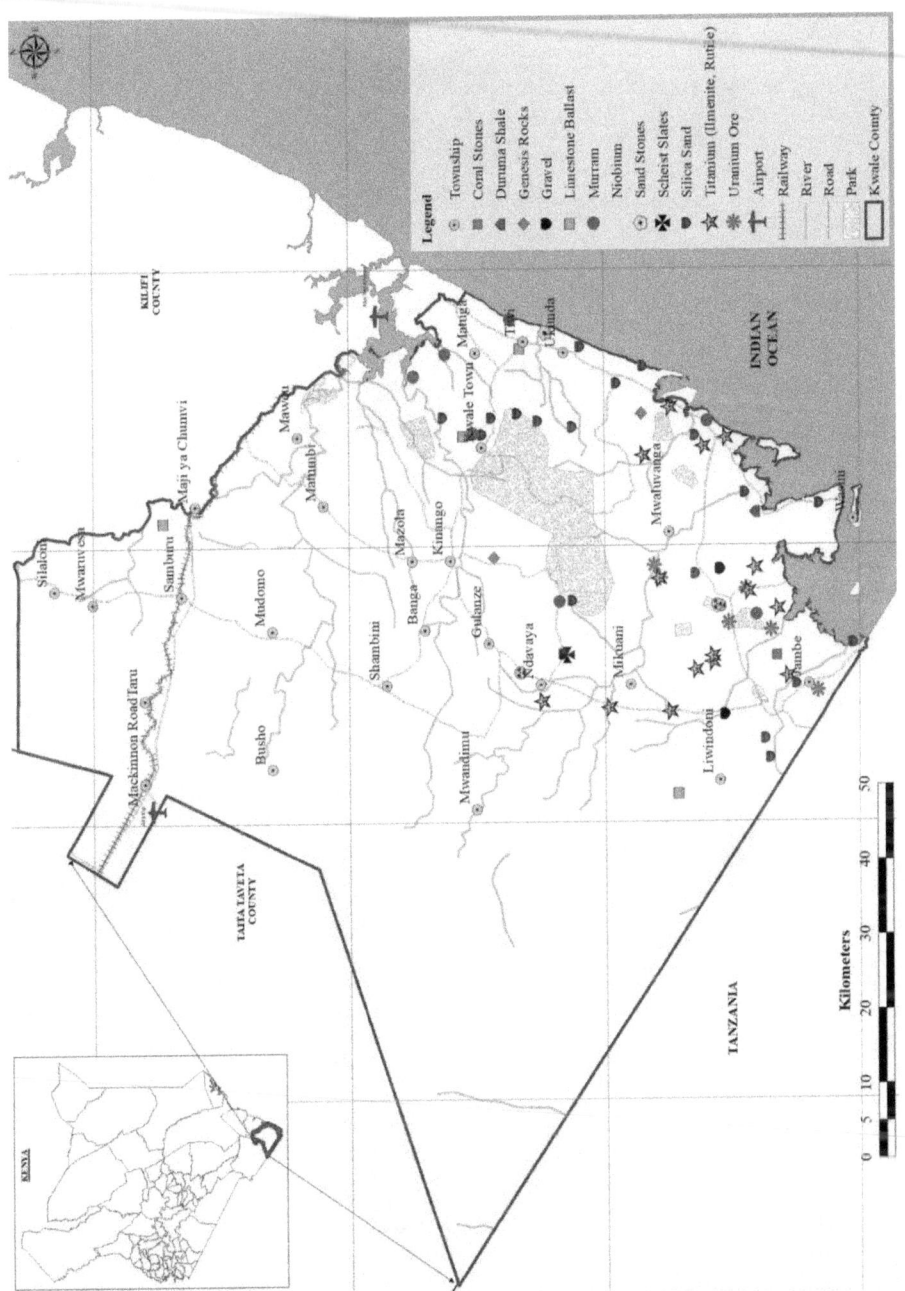

Source: https://www.google.com/search?client=firefox-b-d&q=map+of+kwale+county. Accessed on 08/02/2020: 4.51 pm East African Time

Chapter 1

Itineration in the Digo Country[1]: July 16-28, 1912

By Rev. Geo. W. Wright

"This is an original report made by CMS missionary Rev. George Wright after a trip into Digo land in 1912. It helps give voice to the missionaries and their experiences at the beginning of the mission period this book is discussing."

The men who were with me were an interesting collection. The medico was Sheikh Aliah Bankuh, one of the late Dr. Pennell's[2] converts, a Pathan,[3] who had been taught medical work in the Bannu Hospital. He had been sent to us as part of a sense Dr. Pennell had for evangelizing Indians who have left their own country. This I gathered from Aliah B. in our tent during the journey. If all those who came under Dr. Pennell's influence revere him as our man does, then the Doctor's memory is a "sweet savour" indeed.

---

[1] This typed manuscript is from the microfilm of the Church Missionary Society Archive (published by Adam Matthew), Section IV Africa Mission, Part 18 Kenya Mission, Reel 367, retrieved at Asbury Theological Seminary, Wilmore, Kentucky. It portrays in their own words some of the perspectives of the early CMS missionaries to Digo land, and was written by Rev. George W. Wright, who was posted at Mombasa. It was written August 18, 1912.
[2] Dr. Theodore Leighton Pennell (1867-1912) was a missionary doctor for the CMS who worked in hospitals in what in now Pakistan.
[3] A native group in Afghanistan

Our next man is a Catechist, an African of the coast district. The name of his country is Duruma. He was of the greatest use. For besides his own Duruma tongue, he converses readily in Digo, Swahili, Hindustani, Giryama, and English. The English he used sometimes in order to help us, but the others were all necessary to us as we passed in and out among the people. We had been told that the whole of the people know our Mombasa language, Swahili. That was not so. Along the main road it was so, but away from it very little Swahili was really known. It was this which made Catechist Paul invaluable. The country is supposed to be Digo, but we found also people of Giryama, which is north of Mombasa, of Paul's own country Duruma, others of Jambani,[4] 100 miles inland, also some Hindu speakers.

Our porters were all Christians, baptised or catechumens. One was an old freed slave, who had been, as cook, with Bishop Tucker to Uganda. One was a Kikuyu, two others Wakamba, and the last a Kavirondo. All these men were from interior Africa. It was a great benefit to have all Christians, for they understood what we were about, joined us in prayer about the work, and helped us with the services when we were camped at any village.

Our first day's march was a long one. The men themselves chose this. They had friends at Gasi, which is a coconut plantation, 27 miles south of Mombasa, the present centre of thousands of acres of splendid land, which had been leased by the Protectorate Government to the East Africa Estates, Limited. The intention of the present company, one gathers, is to plant different areas, and sub-let them to subsidiary companies or to private persons. This had already been done with a large area of rubber.

On these two estates three of our Christian lads with their wives are living. All occupy positions of some authority. All have good reports from their European masters. They are helping the labourers in the estates as far as they can. They find that many want to learn. The labourers are men from the interior tribes, chiefly Kikuyu from the slopes of Mount Kenia. Our arrival after the long hot journey of 27 miles or so found us too tired to do anything but get to rest as quickly as possible. We had aimed to do this piece of the road quickly as our men

---

4 This word is not clear in the original, so it may be incorrectly written.

had on two previous occasions visited this part of the country, whereas our object was to reach the unevangelised, and to spy out the country for possibilities of future work.

On our way we had sold one Gospel, and given away another to a Mohammadan who had been very kind to some of our party on a previous visit. As soon as possible on the next day, we went along to the village of Gasi. This is a Mohammadan centre, and has a very bad name for immorality. It was the centre of the supporters of Moaruk, a Mohammadan rebel, who gave some trouble to the authorities in 1895. His rebellion left the Digo country in a very unsettled state, whose effects have continued until very recently. The country is a splendid one for coconuts, but the people are only now beginning to plant in any quantity. There are many signs of deserted plantations. Again, the people are now beginning to come out of the hills to which they fled during the troubles, and the country is giving promise of becoming populous, but it will be some years yet before the many gaps are filled up.

On a previous visit we had had a splendid opportunity of reading to the Elders of Gasi, and reasoning with them out of the Scriptures. They had pressed us to come again, and had asked for a teacher. This time we had a further opportunity of pointing them to their true Saviour, reading to them, at the request of one of their number, the account of the Crucifixion. Then they wanted the account of the Resurrection. We read that to them. Some asked foolish questions, but the great majority of them were attentive listeners. They acknowledged they were sinners, and we were able to plainly point them to the only Way of Salvation. It is very noticeable how they listen respectfully to the Word read. The spoken word has much less respectful hearing. We were able to sell four Gospels. The men promised to consider the building of a house for a teacher, which we made a condition as showing whether they were in earnest or not.

Leaving Gasi in the early afternoon, we were able to reach a group of villages called Msambweni. Our medico, our cook, and two tired porters were left to give out medicines to all-comers, and to cook the evening meal while the remainder of us went round the villages. As it was round evening and by this time the men had all returned from their fishing, the chief means of livelihood, we were able to reach them. We found earnest listeners at all the places, and had not darkness overtaken us we should have been able to do much more. Not a soul could read, so we were unable to sell books. Fortunately the next morning we had a patient who had been at our Mzizima Hospital some years ago, and who still remembered his letters, which he had been taught there. Much to the astonishment of the people he was able to spell slowly some texts we had with us, and leaving some of these we urged him to teach his companions. The next morning on reaching the crossing of the river Ramisi, over which, because of the crocodiles, we had to be paddled, we had an opportunity of a long talk with two Baganda, one of whom is the ferryman. His companion was a sufferer with open ugly sores, and we were able to tell him the news of the Love of God, who had sent His Son, with healing for spirit as well as body. They said it was "Good News."

One part of my own work was to see several Englishmen who are living a very isolated life in the Digo country. Three of these I saw at the Gasi plantations, and had what I hope was a helpful time with them. Something you cannot possibly realize, without coming out and being with them for a time, what a terrible isolation this settler life is. This is especially so in the fever-stricken Coast district. Everything about the man is dead against him, and even the most experienced of them will tell you how hard to bear the isolation is at times. It was a great joy, therefore, to be able to combine Chaplaincy and Missionary work. Our halting place after leaving the Ramisi was the *shamba* (i.e. plantation) of one of these friends and, as at Gasi, we got a right hearty welcome. The next morning we were off for the one Government Station of this district. It is called Shimoni. It has a series of caves or holes. In the Swahili language "ni" means a place, and "shimo" a hole or deep cavity. So the natives call the Station "Shimoni." The officer in charge was away visiting some of his outlying places. We had reluctantly to leave without seeing him. We were able to sell eight Gospels before we were very kindly taken by the Government boat to our next objective, Vanga.

At Shimoni we had the pleasure of being reminded how we are building on another's foundation. One of the clerks told how, in Mombasa, he had heard Mr. Taylor, Mrs. Burt, and had been at Mr. Parker's school. He was one who bought a portion of Scripture, and would have bought more had we had with us a wider selection. We had little opportunity of teaching, as there are no villages near. There is one sign of the cost of

Empire, in two neatly kept graves of young Englishmen, one a soldier who was killed during the "Moaruk" rebellion, and the other a young District Officer who died at this most lonely station. A two hours' sail took us past the Island of Waseen,[5] visited by Dr. Krapf and Mr. Taylor, to the town of Vanga, the sorthernmost point of British East Africa, and but a walk of a few minutes to the British and German East African border.

Vanga is a Mohammadan town of just over 600 well-built houses, well kept, and prosperous. It is a rice-growing district, possibly somewhat unhealthy in the rainy season. When we landed at four in the afternoon we found the local governor, the *liwali*, in his office with a large band of the Elders of the place. He asked us our business. We told him we were going through the country to teach the people about God. "Very good," he said, "we are all the slaves of God." "Ah," we rejoined, "this is just the difference; we are here to tell you all that we are 'sons of God.'" This led to reading from the New Testament, a walk with the *liwali* to be shown the town and sleeping quarters, a cup of tea and sweet rice cakes, and an appointment for the next morning when the people might gather together to hear more of our teaching. In the meantime, our men were selling portions of Scripture.

Our meeting place next morning was the spacious marketplace. There we reasoned with them from the Scriptures, knowing them now as claiming to be children of Abraham their *privilege* was to proclaim the Gospel to the whole world, and not to leave it to us who had been grafted into the "olive tree." We left later with a guide given us by the *liwali*, a pressing invitation to come again, and if possible bring with us the means of starting School and Hospital.

As a strategic point, Vanga is one of the best. Close to the border, on the main Coast Road, with at least three open, well-trodden roads from the interior converging on it, with a fine harbor into which the River Umba empties itself, the centre of a rice and mangrove bark area, with a people, some Mohammadan and others heathen, open and willing to hear the Gospel, the town should prove a fruitful field. Around it and within easy reach are many villages. The *liwali* expects fifty more houses to be built in the town during the year, its growth is so rapid. Will

---

[5] Probably Wasini Island.

you please pray that we may enter in and be much blessed there? The remainder of our day after leaving Vanga was spent in going from village to village, teaching and doing what we could to heal their diseases. In one small place we had 13 patients. In all the villages we found someone needing medical help.

The evening found us entering an old stockaded village in the centre of elephant country. We had passed many tracks during the day, and our guides had showed us some of the damage the herds had done. Nziriwe,[6] the village we had reached, was also interesting in having an old flagpole, erected by a German officer during the scrabble for land in the eighties, but which had proved to be on the British side of the border when matters were settled. Here we saw a curious atmospheric effect. The village was in dense bush, and on a slope. Our campfire was at the lower end of the village near the doubly stockaded entrance. After our meal, the boys and girls of the place who were unmarried began to make a fire near a hut but close to us. In this hut we learned they would all sleep, it being the custom of the Digo people to put the unmarried people into such a separate hut. There being a moon until about 11:00 p.m., the young people proceeded to dance about the fire, and in and around the nearer huts until the waning of the light of the moon sent them off to rest. As they ran to and fro their figures in the moon and firelight assumed gigantic proportions, so that one was reminded of the stories of our Northern giants and their forest homes. We thought we should be allowed to rest when the young people were gone. In a short time, however, we heard an unearthly yelling and in a few minutes a band of men appeared dancing, shrieking, singing. Arranging themselves in rows they sang a kind of wild Gregorian chant until joined by those of the village who would accompany them to other villages, and finally to an appointed centre where the noise of a beaten drum told us through the night that one of the tribal dances was being carried on. As many of these dances are abominable, they are a great obstruction to our work.

This place, Nziriwe, was one of the most barren in result. A conversation with a group of men, medicine to four people, two picture texts left with them was all we could do. During the day after leaving Nziriwe we followed the border for a few hours, and then struck inland. It was Saturday and we were on the lookout for a good centre for Sunday

---

[6] Possibly Dzirive.

work. This we found in a range of hills called Mwena, a place where four tribes are beginning to mix. It was there that we found out the usefulness of our Catechist, Paul. If we entered a Digo village, or one inhabited by Wakamba, or Waduruma, or Wagiryama Paul was at home with all. Saturday, Sunday, and early Monday we were busy here, there being many villages of the different tribes, though none as yet are very big. The people had never heard the Gospel before, and as they said, "they needed much teaching as they were very ignorant." Many had never seen a white man, and consequently made themselves scarce on our approach to the village. We were given pressing invitations to come and really teach the people.

We were now at the farthest point which, in the time at our disposal, we could reach. We were told that a populous district lay before us,[7] but two days heavy marching through a waterless district gave us a new idea of populousness. We have already mentioned the Moaruk rebellion. Its result was to cause the people to flee into the hills, and leave the plains uncultivated. They are now returning, but it is in ones and twos who settle in such a way that we seldom found a number of houses together. A man brings his wife, or wives, his children, if any, his cattle, sheep, and goats, if those are his wealth, selects his piece of land, builds his house and surrounding hedge to keep away the wild animals. His next-door neighbor may be within sight, or be quite a distance away. There seem to be no rules to observe. It will be different after a few years of peaceful settlement. Growing families mean more huts clustered round that of the head of the family. In the meantime it means for us a large amount of time taken to effect little, for one may visit village after village only to find that all but the oldest and youngest are away with the flock, or busy in the corn or vegetable patch which, because it must be near the water, may be a very long way from the village.

We left Mwena at daybreak on Monday. Three hours out we had an example of native hospitality, also of their difficulty in getting water. We had come to one of the lonely places I have just mentioned. Our men were very hot and tired and thirsty. The man who owned the house was alone. He had one pot of water partly full. He gave each man a coconut shell full of the precious liquid. Then he told us in answer to our enquiries about water that the nearest was about three hours away.

---

[7] Possibly this could be a reference to current day Lunga-Lunga.

The women had left at 6:00 a.m. for a fresh supply, and had not yet- 9:30 a.m.- returned. About noon we had a hearty welcome from an old man, who with his family has cultivated a large area of ground and has fairly large flocks. He tried to understand that God is his Father. He had heard something of this years ago at Rabai when Mr. Rebmann lived there. This must have been before the year 1873. He badly wanted one of his wives and a little child to have some sores dressed, but the child had fled into the thick scrub with other children when we came near the village, and could not be persuaded to come out, while nothing would persuade the woman to be dressed except by her own womankind.

We rested that night under the welcome shade of a fine old mango tree. A spring of water not far away enriched the neighbourhood, and the owner of Kakoneni,[8] the village close by spring and mango tree, had the houses neatly arranged, and the garden close by carefully kept, quite the exception in such a country as this. We had a good talk here about the Love of God for us, and finding that one boy could read we were able to sell a Gospel. We left under a promise to come again and teach them to read. At 10:00 a.m. we were at one of the big wayside marketplaces[9] just in time to point the buyers and sellers to something that we had, much more precious then their wares, but to be had, "without money and without price." This struck home, and we were carefully listened to. The afternoon found us back on the Coast Road at Msambweni, near the village where we had been welcomed on the previous Tuesday. We had another welcome to other villages, especially from the brother of the patient of our Mzizima Hospital, whose reading of the texts had helped us the previous week. It turned out that those who had listened to our words on the first occasion, had told these men what they had heard. Thus the way is prepared for us.

A night at the Gasi plantation prepared us for a scramble over rocks and cliff paths, indistinguishable to me but apparently open and plain to Catechist Paul, in order to visit two villages we had left to be worked in our return journey. The first place we found everybody at home, a little inclined to be argumentative until they heard some of the

---

[8] This could not possibly be correct, since Kakoneni is north of Mombasa and not in Kwale County, but perhaps the name has changed since 1912. He could have also meant Kikoneni

[9] While not named, this could be Nguruweni, which lies between Kikoneni and Msambweni.

precious Word. We spent a long time with them, reading and explaining the Word of God. Our next village was a long way along the cliffs. We found two old men there, whom we tried to teach. Our way then led us through an old fortification, built no one knew when, but from its great size and rough appearance it seemed to have been built as a refuge by the people into which to flee when the Portuguese under Vasco de Gama and his successors came too near. A few minutes away we found the remains of what seemed to have been an old native town. Another day's march and visiting villages near the road, a quiet night near the house of a man eager to read and hear the Gospel, an early morning march, and we were again in Mombasa, picking up the threads of the work among white and black.

I see that I have not said where Digo is. It is the strip of country south of Mombasa Island to the German border. Its northern border is the long stretches of water which give us at the southern end of Mombasa Island the magnificent Kilindini Harbour, one of the finest in Africa. About twenty miles inland, a long series of ridges ranging from 400 to 1400 feet high form the western boundary. This country is one of the richest parts of the fertile coast strip. It is the Missionary District of our Mombasa congregation, in which we hope to find scope for our energies for the coming years, but especially to bring home to every Christian here the necessity of carrying the Gospel farther afield.

Geo. W. Wright
Aug. 18, 1912

Chapter 2

Culture, Identity and Power in the Digo Mission

By Ferdinand Manjewa M'bwangi

Introduction

While appreciating the critical role of three African scholars whose study from 2006 to 2012 related to the role of communal norms in informing the identity of some Kenyan coastal communities, I must however concede that they did not explore the role of cultural norms in shaping the identity of the people in Digo land. Thus, this chapter attempts to address the question: What role did the Digo cultural practices play in shaping the identity of the community in Digo land? This research has established that during the emergence of the Christian mission in Digo land and thereafter, Digo cultural norms, beliefs, and values played a significant role of maintaining a cultural identity that in turn was instrumental in maintaining cohesion for a multi-religious community. This chapter builds its case first, by briefly reviewing the contributions of Bryson Samboja, Dorcas Mlamba Kiundu, and Tsawe-Munga Chidongo in the study of Kenyan coastal people and also applies Janet Huskinson's cultural identity theory to elaborate cultural identity maintenance, representation, and perception among the people in Digo land.

Previous Research in Kenyan Coastal Communities

The doctoral work of Bryson Samboja, Dorcas Mlamba Kiundu, and Tsawe-Munga Chidongo collectively provide the secondary literature for this chapter regarding research on Kenyan coastal communities. These three scholars collected data from the coast of Kenya and discussed the cultural issues of the indigenous people, where the Mijikenda form a majority of the population. The Digo people are part of the larger Mijikenda community. Digo land falls within the Kwale area where the two main Mijikenda clans, the Digo and the Duruma, form the majority. While Dorcas Mlamba's study covers the Genesis creation accounts, Samboja focuses on the use of *Hirizi* charms among the Muslims. Chidongo's research is mainly concerned with dialogue between African Indigenous Religion and Christianity. These three scholars employ a qualitative research design with the oral interview as a technique for collecting data from the field. The coastal cultural values provide the point of departure for their study, as will be explained below.

B.K. Samboja (2005)

In his doctoral thesis, "Muslims Use of *Hirizi* charms in Mombasa, Kenya, and its Implications for the Christian Mission" (2005), Samboja addresses the problem of real and/or imagined power behind *hirizi* charms and the resources of power available through Christ (Samboja 2005: 4). With this problem in mind, Samboja's research is guided by the question of how *hirizi* charms are used in Mombasa and the implications for the Christian mission. Part of Samboja's findings, which closely border on the role of cultural values in identity formation, is that "Islam allows the practice of polygamous marriage... [and] is more accommodating to traditional [use of charms] more than mission churches" (Samboja 2005: 192). From Samboja's findings, it emerges that those African traditional religious values, such as the use of *hirizi* charms whose use, as Samboja (2005) notes, is more likely to be approved in Islam than in Christianity, form part of religious norms and beliefs that benchmark identity in some Kenyan coastal communities which include the Mijikenda.

Dorcas C. Mlamba (2006)

Dorcas C. Mlamba, who earned an additional name after marrying Mr. Peter Kiundu, is referred to here as Mlamba Kiundu. In her PhD thesis, "The Woman God Created: Some Cultural Implications for Coastal Bantu People," she divulges a research undertaking provoked by a remark made by fellow male clergy during a conference that "the Bible has placed the woman in the kitchen and that is her divine place" (Mlamba 2006: 1). This observation from Mlamba's conversation with fellow male clergy betrays her concern for male chauvinism in the church. Coupled with her response that "it was evident that I was intruding on men's territory," her resistance against long overdue cultural injustice against women calls for scholarly engagement. Her findings are revealed; and articulated in the rest of her PhD thesis. Consequently, Mlamba embarks on research guided by the question; "What is the identity of the Woman God created?" (Mlamba 2006: 2). To answer this question, Mlamba undertakes an exegetical study of the Genesis creation accounts (Gen 1-3), which is viewed in the cultural context of the ancient Israelite family and the place of a woman in the African traditional family. In pursuit of her curious investigation, Mlamba found that the social predicament of a woman is compounded by three cultural layers; (1) Bantu coastal norms were instilled in individuals as they are borne and nurtured into maturity; (2) The presence of a colonial layer associated with a missionary reading of the Bible and, (3) the Jewish/Israelite culture of the biblical text itself (Mlamba 2006: 4). Given Mlamba's findings, the cultural influence on identity nuanced in Samboja's research on identity formation is now clarified. Mlamba's thesis has made it clear that the cultural norms and beliefs that influence our perception of the identity of others are not so much based on an individuals' choice, but are a result of a process of communal socialization. Thus, Mlamba's thesis demonstrates the role of cultural norms in shaping the identity of women in the region.

Tsawe-Munga Chidongo (2012)

Writing six years after Mlamba, Tsawe-Munga Chidongo, in his PhD thesis, "Exploring Dialogue: Reflections on Christianity's Mission and African Indigenous Religion" (2012), specifically addresses the role of African culture and Christianity by exploring the relationship between Christianity and African Indigenous Religions (AIR) with the overall purpose of discovering "whether at the height of successive problems in Africa, AIR and Christianity can agree to cooperate and together build and heal society" (Chidongo 2012: i). Furthermore, Chidongo's observation that the adherents of African indigenous religion "being themselves exclusivist by regarding their religion, culture and tradition as superior, are reluctant to accept the religious supremacy of the Europeans." He discusses the cultural power of AIR in resisting a certain cultural influence from a people perceived as foreigners. This assumption is further reinforced by the popular belief among the Mizdi-Chenda (also called Mijikenda), as noted by Chidongo, that "he who abandons his culture and traditions is a slave of the other (*mricha chikw'ao ni mtumwa*)" (Chidongo 2012: 50).

Given the studies conducted by Samboja, Mlamba and Chidongo, we can deduce that the Kenyan coastal cultures, whether in terms of the use of *hirizi* charms, male chauvinism against women, or the use of African indigenous religious values that resist foreign influence, have an impact on the perception of identity among the coastal people of Kenya. This assumption provokes the following question that I attempt to answer in this chapter: How far did culture contribute to the formation of identity during the emergence of missionary Christianity in Digo land in the early 20th Century and beyond? Guided by the search for an answer to this question, I propose the following argument: during the emergence of missionaries in Digo land (the myth of origin), Digo African indigenous beliefs and norms along with Christian beliefs, represented, and facilitated the maintenance, perception, and formation of the cultural identity of the people. From this point I will proceed by first outlining Huskinson's (2009) cultural identity theory in order to acquire an interpretative lens for explaining the maintenance, representation and perception of cultural identity. Using this theory in Digo land in the early 20th Century, I will explore cultural identity, Christian identity and power relations in Digo land.

Janet Huskinson's Cultural Identity Theory

In her book-chapter, "Looking for Identity, Culture and Power" (2009), Janet Huskinson outlines three ways in which people in the first century CE experienced Rome's political power. First, Huskinson (2009) says that they experienced Rome's political power as a representation of its cultural values. In this case, personification and the Romans' ancestral customs and beliefs played a significant role in symbolizing peoples' status and conceptualization of relationships in response to Rome's political power (Huskinson 2009: 7-9). Second, Huskinson (2009) observed that peoples' identity, in terms of group membership, was demonstrated by shared cultural values. Peoples' cultural identity was expressed through essential attributes of identity such as ethnicity, language, and beliefs, to suggest the existence of a "homogenous identifiable Roman culture" (Huskinson 2009: 11-12; 15-16). Third, Huskinson (2009) asserts that when we keenly analyse the contextual cultural representation in the Roman Empire in terms of their motives, power relations begin to emerge. These power relations are further categorized into social power and ideological power of the people in terms of the relations between the Romans with Rome as the center of the political power and the elites as the mediators of this power. This power relation between Rome and the provinces underscores the essence of "Romanization" (Huskinson 2009: 19-22). In what follows, I will attempt to draw from Huskinson's cultural identity theory to elaborate the maintenance, representation, and perception of a cultural identity during the emergence of Christianity in Digo land in the early 20th Century.

Maintenance, Representation, and Perception of Cultural Identity

Digo land is that part of Kenya, currently known as Kwale County, located in the Southern part of the Kenyan (or the East African) coast. Ethnically, in the early 20th century, the population of Digo land was mainly composed of two Mijikenda sub-clans; the Digo and Duruma communities. Although the concern of this chapter is to discuss cultural identity in Digo land, a little bit of the historical emergence of Christian missionaries in the early 20th century is crucial to mention because Christian identity forms part of the discussion of the chapter. During a recent oral interview conducted at Kwale on October 10, 2018, Mzee Shadrack Mwalonya (2018) told us that Christianity was first introduced in Digo land in 1902 by the Reverends Binns and Bans who were stationed at the Freretown mission station, Kisauni Mombasa. In a follow up visit in 1904 by Binns and Banns, Mzee Dundu, the grandfather of Ven. Elijah Ramtu, donated a parcel of his land for the construction of a church at Viongwani village, Kwale, though he was and remained a Muslim throughout his life. According to Elijah Ramtu (2018), in around 1910 the beacon of the church in Viongwani was laid down by Binns and Bans. Shadrack Mwalonya noted that in 1914 Rev. George Wright, who was also visiting Viongwani from Freretown, constructed the first church at Viongwani. In the years that followed, the first people to convert to Christianity are the descendants of Mzee Dundu. These descendants of Mzee Dundu include: Samuel Maneno, Elijah Ramtu, and Shadrack Mwalonya, some of whom formed part of the focus discussion group (FDG) in the course of this research.

In this chapter, *culture* is to be understood as "shared meanings" composed of "common assumptions, and experiences...expressed by following certain common practices" and *identity* is "described as a way of placing people-individuals or communities-within a particular cultural context" (Huskinson 2009: 5). Thus '*cultural identity*' is defined as group identity grounded on common and shared norms, beliefs, and values. Thus, 'Digo cultural identity' entails the identity of the Digo community as shaped by Digo indigenous religious norms, beliefs, and values. Similarly, 'Christian identity' refers to a cultural identity of the Digo that is shaped by Christian norms, beliefs, and values, particularly as imparted by the early missionaries in Digo land. Having explored the emergence of Christianity in Digo land and the definition of cultural identity, we now focus on the identity formation in Digo land during the arrival of the missionaries.

Cultural Identity in Digo Land

During and even after the arrival of Christian missionaries in Digo land, the formation of the cultural identity of the Digo people was based on myths of origin and Digo indigenous religious traditional norms and beliefs. The popular myth of Shungwaya is used to explain the origins of the Digo people as well as the Duruma. On one hand, Shungwaya is said to be the great grandfather of the Mijikenda because from his 9 sons, come the nine sub-clans (Digo, Duruma, Rabai, Ribe, Kauma, Giriama, Chonyi, Kambe and Jibana) that constitute the Mijikenda community, emerged. On the other hand, there is a Mrima-Mumwezi myth that tells of the origin of the Duruma. According to Mzee Munga Wa-Mumbo (2018), two brothers, Mrima and Mumwezi, once decided, during the great famine in Kinango, to visit Shungwaya to seek employment. Luckily while at Shungwaya, they were employed by a wealthy Digo man as cattle keepers. The Digo man paid Mrima and Mumwezi their cattle keeping wages by marrying off two of his daughters. Having received their dues, Mrima and Mumwezi set off to return to Kinango, also known as 'Duruma land', to settle down and begin their own families. The descendants of Mrima and Mumwezi constitute the main clans among the Duruma people in Kinango. This Mrima-Mumwezi myth was primarily used to explain the formation of the identity of the Duruma by conceptualizing a relationship between the Duruma and the Digo. The Mrima-Mumwezi myth underscores the cultural identity of the Duruma as nephews of the Digo on the one hand, and on the other hand, the Digo are by default the maternal (not paternal) uncles of the Duruma. Furthermore, grounding the relations between the Digo and Duruma in the Mrima-Mumwezi myth depicts a representation of a cultural identity through personification. While in the case of the Roman Empire, cultural identity was experienced in terms of personification through iconographic representation such as mosaic floor tiles (Huskinson 2009: 7–8), in the case of the Mrima-Mumwezi myth, cultural identity was construed through personification symbolized by the relationship between Mdigo and Muduruma. This is to say, on account of Mrima-Mumwezi, Mdigo is a personification of a maternal uncle just as Muduruma is a personification of a nephew to the Digo. This symbolic personification between the Digo and Duruma underscores power relations between the Digo and Duruma by providing a relationship between these two sub-clans of the Mijikenda as already negotiated by the Mrima-Mumwezi myth to transcend biological limitations.

Besides the maternal relations and the Mrima-Mumwezi myth, Digo traditional custom underscores biological relations between a nephew and his uncles. The uncle-nephew relations among the Digo depicts the power relations secured by maternal relations. According to Samuel Maneno (2018), Digo maternal relations obligate the uncles to pay for the nephews' dowry before marriage. If a nephew is fined by the community for committing any offense, maternal uncles of that particular person are tasked with the responsibility of paying the fine on behalf of their nephew. Similarly, nephews are entitled to a share of their maternal uncle's inheritance.

In addition to traditional customs, the formation of cultural identity in Digo land is provided by Digo religio-indigenous norms and beliefs. To this end, Digo burial rites, known as "Kuoga-Maji" (ritual washing) are important in depicting the relationship between living and dead relatives. During the recent interviews at Kwale, Samuel Maneno (2018) told us that: *"wakati wa kuzika, wadigo halisi wana siku ya kuoga maji ambayo lengo lake huwa ni kufukuza kifo na kuzuia aliekufa asiwaandame jamaa zake walio hai,"* ("during burial, traditionally the Digo performed a body-washing ritual whose purpose was to dispel death and to restrain the departed soul from haunting their own living relatives.") According to Ramtu (2018), the "Kuoga-Maji" burial rite is performed on the grave side of a previously buried relative. During this ceremony, water is sprinkled on the relatives of the dead and is done in such a manner that it falls directly on the grave of the departed relative. The purpose of this burial rite as told by Samuel Maneno (2018) and confirmed by Elijah Ramtu (2018), is to dispel the spirit of death from the relatives of the dead as well as to prevent the spirit of the dead from coming back to haunt the relatives of the dead person. Thus, this kind of burial rite is crucial in the maintenance of a traditional Digo cultural identity, because it is customarily understood to safeguard the relations between the living and the departed.

Given the above brief observation of the role of Digo indigenous religious and traditional beliefs and norms in maintaining cultural identity among the Digo and Duruma, it emerges that during their arrival in Digo land in the early 20th Century, Christian missionaries, such as Binns, Bans, and Wright found a community whose social harmony and cohesion had been secured by these traditional and religious beliefs. To attempt to plant a new religion in such a social environment in a manner that attempts to shake the cohesion and harmony of a community secured by these and other traditional and religious beliefs and norms, would most likely result in creating tensions. Some people would probably resist any external influence to protect the cohesion and harmony of their community. In what follows, we shall see how in the context of the existing Digo cultural identity, another cultural identity, introduced through conversion to Christianity, would be accepted and maintained.

Christian Identity in Digo Land

Huskinsons' (2009:15-16) argument that cultural identity has "much to do with the perceptions of other people as with ones' own," entails the description of identity in terms of 'them-us' rhetoric. That means, our perception of who we are, is generated from self-knowledge and/or knowledge of others about us in relation to other people. The recent narratives emerging from oral interviews conducted at Kwale play a significant role in explaining the perception of Christian identity in Digo land in the early 20th century, in terms of "them-us" rhetoric. Narrating the response of early 20th century missionaries in Digo land on some of the traditional norms that shapes Digo cultural identity, Maneno said:

> *Yule mwarabu aliye leta uislam Digo hakumkataza Mdigo kuishi na mila zake, alimruhusu Mdigo aendelee kuwa na wake wengi, jambo ambalo lilionekana kuwa ishara ya utajiri. Waislamu hawakukatazwa kutumia hirizi, au kuenda kwa mganga ili kupungwa pepo. Lakini Wameshinari walikataza haya yote wakiyaona kuwa ni dhambi* (Maneno, 2018).

> *That Arab who brought Islam did not bar the Digo to pursue their culture, he allowed the Digo people to continue practising polygamy, a practice that signified wealthy status. Muslims were not forbidden to use traditional charms or to seek deliverance from diviners. But, missionaries prohibited us from all these practices seeing them as being sinful.* (Maneno, 2018).

Maneno's narrative reveals the possibility of conflict between the Christian beliefs and the Digo traditional cultural values as a result of the missionaries' attempt to convert the people to Christianity. This conflict may have been occasioned by the perception of Christian identity in contrast to Digo cultural beliefs. Following this perception of Christian identity, Samuel Maneno and Elijah Ramtu (2018) told us that after their conversion to Christianity, in order to maintain their Christian identity, they had to reject taking part in some of the Digo cultural practices' including funeral rites such the "*Kuoga-Maji*" and shaving the head, among others. Consequently, Maneno's and Ramtu's (2018) narratives demonstrate the cost of conversion to Christianity. To become a Christian you had to be ready to reject some of the traditional beliefs that were crucial in maintaining a Digo cultural identity.

Furthermore, conversion to Christianity in Digo land to some extent resulted to conflicts with blood relatives who had become Muslims. During the interview, Elijah Ramtu told us that:

> *Nyakati hizo za ukristo kufika Viongwani waliookoka na kuwa wakristo walihitaji wawe wavumilivu. Sisi tuliteswa na kutengwa na jamaa zetu waiokuwa Waislamu. Ilibidi pia kuimarisha ndoa za kikristo kati ya familia ya Zani, Maneno na Ramtu ambao walikuwa wachache sana* (Ramtu, 10.10.2018).

> *During the advent of Christianity in Viongwani those who received salvation to become Christians needed to be resilient. We were persecuted and socially discriminated by our closest relatives who were Muslims. This prompted our families to practice Christian marriages within the three families of Zani, Maneno and Ramtu who were a minority in number* (Ramtu, 2018*)*.

Besides sad tales where converts to Christianity were persecuted by relatives who had converted to Islam, Ramtu's narrative talks about the maintenance of the Christian identity by limiting marriage to the three families of Zani, Maneno, and Ramtu. A curious scenario emerges from Ramtu's narrative. The persecution of Ramtu here probably reveals the conflict between Christian beliefs and Islamic beliefs during the emergence of missionary Christianity in Digo land.

The tensions that characterized the relations of the Muslims, Christians, and the adherents of Digo indigenous religion during the introduction of Christianity in Digo land by Christian missionaries, creates the impression that these conflicts had torn apart the social cohesion in Digo land. But, as we shall see in a short while, in spite of these tensions caused by the introduction of missionary Christianity, certain cultural beliefs and norms held the community together, particularly as demonstrated by the following case of power relations in Viongwani village, in Kwale County.

Power Relations in Digo Land

Huskinson noted that "when we look at the context of cultural representations and their motives, power emerges as a key factor" (Huskinson 2009: 19-22). This motivation is further demonstrated through economic power, social power, and political power. Huskinson's ideological notion of the function of power relations in the Roman Empire in terms of the relationship between Rome and the provinces is pertinent in elaborating power relations in Digo land during the emergence of missionary Christianity.

Consequently, the narratives that have been told during the interviews of Johana Maneno, Lugo Gore, and Nimrod Taabu (2018) are important in explaining power relations in Digo land. Because Johana Maneno and Nimrod Taabu were trained by the Christian missionaries as artisans, they were empowered economically to fend for their family's economic needs, but such training also enabled them to become mobile. At one point Maneno and Taabu travelled from Viongwani to Nairobi to work at King George's Rifles' Military Hospital (now Kenyatta National Hospital) as artisans. Having been trained as catechists, while in Nairobi, both would teach catechism at St. Steven's Anglican Parish, Jogoo Road, Nairobi. It is their identity and roles as artisans and catechists that would demonstrate the notion of power relations. Not only did their identity as artisans and catechists limit how they were to be addressed by their pupils and colleagues in the Church and at the hospital, but also reciprocally, these identities limited of how Maneno and Taabu would relate to people at their place of work. To be addressed either as a catechist and/or an artisan symbolized ones' status of belonging to a particular elite group at that time.

Similarly, Canon Lugo Gore's vocation and mobility also depicts some power relations. When Lugo relocated to Rabai, not only did he have the opportunity to attend to his loneliness by marrying a lady from a Christian family in Rabai, but also his vocation as a catechist probably had become a basis for power relations in the community. Thus, Lugo's vocation as a catechist provided social power because it presented him a position of social influence to his immediate catechumens, as well as indirectly to the descendants of these catechumens, and eventually to the larger Rabai and Jimba communities.

Furthermore, Viongwani village was situated in the context of power relations because it was and still is the place which reconnects members of the community scattered abroad beyond Kwale irrespective of their religious affiliation. Huskinson (2009: 10–12) aptly argues that in Roman culture, representation of shared values, such as ancestral customs, demonstrated the peoples' common membership and therefore their Roman identity. In Viongwani village, shared common cultural values, such as the celebration of Christian festivals and participation in the burial of a member of the community, demonstrates the power of traditional beliefs, norms, and practices in reinforcing a homogenous cultural identity; a cultural identity that was not necessarily shaped by religious values but by common traditional shared values of humanity. Viongwani, like Rome, had become a center of this homogenous cultural identity. This is why, according to Elijah Ramtu (2018) and Samuel Maneno (2018), the descendants of the first three converts: Zani, Maneno, and Ramtu, were located outside Kwale. This included the families of Nimrod Tabu and Lugo Gore. They used to travel annually from outside Kwale to celebrate Christmas, New Year, and Easter festivals.

Viongwani became the center of power relations because of ones' affiliation; not to a particular religious group, but because of their connections to Viongwani as the ancestral land, the land of their forefathers that brought the people to celebrate Christian festivals with all of the community, irrespective of their religious affiliation. Thus in this context, although Christmas and Easter are rightfully Christian festivals, their celebration at Viongwani has been converted into a moment to celebrate communal shared values of belonging together, eating together, and laughing together. Do such celebrations indicate the loss of meaning to Christian identity? On the contrary; rather than losing the meaning of Christianity, these celebrations add flavour that resonates with the incarnational perspective of the Christian mission. By celebrating Christian festivals with all of the cultural groups in Viongwani, Christians are, by imitation, demonstrating the mind of Christ "who, being in the very nature of God, did not consider equality with God something to be used to his own advantage" (Phil 2.6).

Conclusion

By focusing on the research of Bryson Samboja (2005), Dorcas Mlamba Kiundu (2006) and Tsawe-Munga Chidongo (2012), this chapter has contributed to the scholarly discussions on the cultures of Kenyan coastal communities. Janet Huskinson's cultural identity theory has enabled this chapter to add new horizons to the study of Kenyan coastal communities by empowering me to discuss the dynamics of cultural identity in Digo land during and after the emergence of Christian missionaries. Digo cultural norms, beliefs, and values have played a significant role in elaborating the maintenance, representation, and perception of cultural identity in Digo land. Although the term cultural identity entails the exploration of all of the religious and other groups in Digo land, this chapter has not explored identity formation among the Muslim community in Digo land. Thus, this chapter provides a platform for future study that can focus on exploring cultural beliefs, norms, and values of Islam in shaping cultural identity in Digo land.

Chapter 3

First European Missionaries in Digo Land
By Bryson K. Samboja

Introduction

Digo land, in Kwale County, is to the south of Mombasa. Mombasa Island was originally known as Mvita Island. The word "vita" in Kiswahili means "war" and this small town was called Mvita because of the wars that had occurred in the town for many years, long before the arrival of the Portuguese in the 16th century CE. The real Mombasa, says Harris (in Samboja 1996), is the old part of the town which is now known as Mji-wa-Kale (Old Town). This was the main center where the slaves were hidden and later sold (Samboja 1996).

If ever we can speak of Christian missionaries before 1844, we refer to the Portuguese conquest in the 16th century. Nthamburi (1991) records that the first missionary outreach in the coastal region of Kenya was by Augustinians who claimed 600 converts in Mombasa, most of whom were the adherents of the traditional religion. It is said that Augustinian Friars had built a church on Mombasa Island. Other churches were built by the Portuguese. Many authors are in consensus that this mission was shortlived because there was a massacre of Christians by the Sultan of Mombasa, Yusuf Bin Hassan (1606-38). He first expelled the former Portuguese masters before he forcibly reconverted all Christian converts to Islam or killed them. Nthamburi (1991) thinks that this kind of action was due to the colonial uprising and the question of subjection.

There is however an argument about this; some think that it was a contest between Islam and Christianity. Nthamburi (1991) picks up Richard Reusch's suggestion that what provoked Yusuf was a Portuguese man's attitude of attempting to take one of his wives as a concubine. This has been refuted by some scholars for lack of evidence. The question of subjection and paternalism was in the minds of early missionaries from the beginning and has continued for many years after. Decisions would be made without consulting any African because to a European they were just savages (Aldephoi 1953: 18).

The golden opportunity to convert the indigenous people to Christianity was lost due to the unethical behavior and through cruelty, oppression, and indulgence in selfish passion, by the Portuguese. After the Arabs regained control in 1729, there was no record of a Christian presence in Mombasa apart from a handful of Goan Christians, who of course were not indigenous. This reveals how one mission approach can create an image that might denote a different cultural perspective leading to misjudging one another (Samboja 1996).

The African Perceptions of Missionaries

Christianity came to the East African shores almost at the same time as the invaders. The natives suspected that the two were one and the same (Welbourn1965: 63). Could this be another reason why Christianity did not take root in Mombasa and instead moved to the interior? Africans, as James Ngugi puts it, would just wonder why Europeans left their homeland, a place of learning, to come to the jungle of Africa. Was this not foolishness? (Ngugi 1964:5). What really was in the minds of these missionaries that they understood Africans either a positive or negative attitude? Krapfs' aim, as we read in his book: *Travels and Missionary Labor in East Africa*, was to introduce civilization and Christianity in the continent of Africa. The question as to why the coast was resistant to the gospel could probably be explained by a comment that Krapf made when talking about the shape of the world as being round. Due to this statement, a Muslim became very indignant and warned the passersby against doctrines that contradicted the Qur'an (Dawson 1887:285).

The Silent Years

It took more than 300 years to again hear of Christian mission in Mombasa. This reminds me of the intertestamental period; the 400 biblical years of silence between the Old Testament and the New Testament. These are the years when God did not speak to the Jewish people till the coming of John the Baptist, the Messiah's forerunner. It took over 300 years from the first converts in Mombasa till the coming of the first recognized missionaries in Mombasa. These missionaries were CMS representatives, Rev. John Ludwig Krapf - a German Lutheran who arrived in Mombasa in 1844; who was followed by the Rev. Johannes Rebmann in 1846, and in 1849 by Jacob Erhardt and J. Wagner. Krapf was given a permit by Sultan Sayyid Said to start a mission station at the coastal city of Mombasa. Soon after his arrival, his wife Rosine and daughter died from malaria (Adam Matthew Digital, 1896: 67-76). On the occasion of his wife's death, Krapf wrote to what is today the Mission Society Committee,

> Tell our friends at home that there is now on the East African Coast a lonely missionary grave. This is a sign that you have commenced the struggle with this part of the world and as the victories of the church are gained by stepping over the graves of her members, you may be the more convinced that the hour is at hand when you are summoned to the conversion of Africa from the Eastern shore (Philp.1936.11).

After this catastrophe, Krapf moved to the higher grounds of Rabai on the coastal hills, which is about 12 miles northwest of the city of Mombasa and started his station in New Rabai (Rabai Mpya). Krapf pioneered work in languages, being the first to produce a Swahili dictionary and to translate the Bible. Within two years, the whole of the New Testament had been translated into Kiswahili (Samboja 1996: 8-9). Through Krapfs' famous book, *Travels, Researches and Missionary Labors*, Methodists were inspired to start work in Kenya. Krapf encouraged the Methodist church to seize the opportunity while the climate was favorable. So, in 1862, he returned to Mombasa to help Thomas Wakefield, the first missionary of the United Methodist Free Church to establish a mission station at Ribe. Wakefield managed to set up mission stations in Ganjoni

(Mazeras), and Jomvu in 1878, a daring thing to do in the middle of the Muslim community, and then later he left to Chonyi (Samboja 1996: 10). They were followed by many other missionaries including Rev. and Mrs. Binns, and J. A. Wray, who arrived in Mombasa in 1882. The vision of the early missionaries seemed to have been changed by Sir Bartle Frere who encouraged Christian missions to concentrate on a settlement of freed slaves at Kisauni in 1875, which came to be known as Freretown (Nthamburi 1991:9). The missionaries were now more occupied with the care of the freed slaves than evangelism. Missionaries were later accused of encouraging the slave trade as well as mistreating the freed slaves. This happened out of the kindness of their hearts as they started to buy slaves from the slave traders in order to free them, and to have them trained and 'disciplined' (Welbourn 1965:66). By 1900, the authorities of the mission believed that the time had come to establish mission centers in the coastal region.

First European Missionaries in Digo

Who are the Digo people? The Digo people are among the nine sub-groups living along the coastal strip of Kenya in East Africa known as the Mijikenda (literally "Nine sub-groups"). Although they speak Chidigo as their mother tongue, most of them understand and speak Kiswahili. Their population is estimated to be 383,053 people (Kenya web.com2001). They are mostly concentrated in the coastal region of Kenya between Mombasa and the border of Tanzania. The Digo have embraced Islam more than any of the other Mijikenda sub-ethnic groups. Nevertheless, the majority have no real knowledge of the Qur'an, in spite of the fact that a few have studied Islam and the Qur'an as a whole. Due to the trade with Muslim Arabs, the Digo people have adopted not only the Muslim Arabian attire, but also their diet. Most Digo women wear long robes and black veils to cover their head when leaving their homes, though some do it without any religious justification apart from the mere attempt to show respect to their husbands. While at home, they normally wear *lesos* that are wrapped around their waists and add another one on their shoulders. Men on the other hand, wear long white robes and a white hat. Most Digos are traders, but they also practice small-scale farming. As far as religious practices are concerned, one would say that the majority of the Digo people are deeply engaged in spiritism and folk Islam (Sesi 2003:13). In 1904, Bans and Binns from Freretown moved to the south coast. In particular, Rev. Bans with three helpers, Machache Baraka from Rabai together with two Kikuyus, Njuguna and Mnuvemupe, went to a place that came to be known as Zungu, where they settled. It is here that Bans built his own house, church, and a teacher's house. He went ahead and constructed a water-borehole at Mwangala. He also brought another person, Efrahim Yamungu, who started cattle farming.

Bans embarked on educating the Digos in his newfound school. Among those he taught, Mwangauchi became the first disciple in the whole of Digo land. Afterwards, Mwazani, Lunganzi, and Gude Zani and others joined (Zani 1983). By May 1910, beacons were put on the Zungu plot (Ramtu 2018). Bans stayed at Zungu for 4 years, and later left for an interior/upcountry mission, claiming that the mission among the Digo was difficult and too challenging for him. After he left, the students were left without a teacher, but Mwangauchi was left in charge of the Zungu projects. By 1913, all the houses were burnt down by a fire Mwagauchi lit on his piece of land. At this time, Rev. Binns was at Freretown in Kisauni. After the fire incident, he received first-hand information from Mwagauchi who was instructed to return while the missionaries consulted together. On his return, Mwagauchi was advised by his brothers to leave because these whites were going to sell him. So, he ran away out of fear for his life, and the Zungu missionary centre in Digo land was left without a substantive caretaker.

During the First World War (1914-18), another European missionary by the name of George Wright came from Freretown, Kisauni. He started planting churches in Digo land. He planted churches in the following areas: Matuga, Vuga, Vyongwani, Golini, Mwachiga, and Yapha. In each of these stations he placed a teacher. Matuga was under teacher Andrew Charles, and then Wright moved to Vuga where he put in place two teachers; namely, Samuel Mathew and Samuel Kiali. He then moved to Vyongwani where he built the church. To his surprise, he discovered that Gude Zani knew how to read and write. Wright resolved not to bring any teacher from outside the area, but to authorize Gude Zani to be in charge. From here, Wright climbed the hills to Golini at Mwachangoma where he built another church. He put Charles Ndundi, a Giriama, as the person in-charge. He was very ambitious, bold, and determined to see to it that the Digo mission was a success. From here, Wright noticed that Lunganzi also knew how to read and write, so he put him in charge as well. All these mighty activities show the great work of Rev. George Wright (Zani 1983).

From Mwachinga, Wright moved to Yapha and planted a church. He found Mwazani who also knew how to write and read the Bible and made him the teacher in charge. During this time, the First World War broke out. It was between the Germans and the British, especially in how it impacted East Africa, as the Germans occupied present day Tanzania. All of the churches except two which George Wright had planted failed. The two that remained were Matuga and Vyongwani. There was good progress at the Matuga church as it saw six people receiving baptism, namely: Joseph Ramtu, Henry Mwamsena Mnono, Paul Mwazimu, Johana Mwapunganisi, Mary Nkuweha, and Grace Nirasiwa. The war also affected the progress at Vyongwani. All the students were taken out of school to join the war. The white missionaries who came instructed that schools be built at Kwale, Tsimba and, Golini (Zani 1983).

After the first arrival of the early white missionaries, there was another period of silence which went by without seeing or hearing of European missionaries in Digo land. Then in the late 1970s and early 1980s, there was a great movement of European missionaries back to Digo land. People like; Malcolm Heartnail, who in the 1980s settled at Golini. Wayne Richard settled at Vuga. He intially stayed with Rev. Rodgers Ziro at Vyongwani. Richard Barnoon settled at Matuga, and Gary Morgan at Tiwi. Malcolm Heartnail was followed by Richard Mang in the 1980s, who left because his work permit came to an end. These Whites/Europeans were conservative Baptists. Wayne Richards was a member of the African Inland Church (AIC). After his permit ended, he left Digo land but came back through Tanzania later. McDougall was also working in Tiwi, but stayed in Tudor (Mwadama 2018).

The Church at Golini in Mwadama's area was not built by Malcolm Heartnail as many thought. It was the work of Sophi Obuya, a Luhya who was sent by the Nairobi Chapel to work among the Digo people. She would be visited by University students who would embark on evangelism among the Digo in Golini. Malcolm Heartnail had constructed a temporary *Makuti* house for worship; which was later burnt down. It was after the burning of the *Makuti* house that they decided to build a permanent Church at Golini. After her contract with the Nairobi

Chapel ended, Obuya went for further studies in Canada where she married a European and did not come back to continue with her work among the Digo. Malcolm Heartnail and Wayne Richard were loved by the Digos because of their overt love and generosity. This enabled them to penetrate deeper into Digo land. In those early days, mission work was not an easy excercise – as some residents would sometimes stone the missionaries' vehicles (Mwadama 2018).

Babu (Grandfather) Joshua and Groceman were Baptist Missionaries in Digoland. Babu Joshua was serving at Tiwi while Groceman was at Golini. They started a fellowship at Mwanzwani School but the community chased them out at one stage, after which Mzee Francis Mwasicho opened a place for them. Soon, the Church flourished despite wrangles in leadership that arose, as each person thought the Europeans would help their side. Consequently, the Church fell apart. Interestingly, these European missionaries were committed to evangelizing Digo land. When Pastor Stephen Chingamba left, Groceman went and prayed with him as he started a fellowship at his home. But that fellowship died down shortly after (Stephen 22.10.18). According to Mwadama, Stephen joined him for a while as he hoped to see the tempers cool down. Groceman gave Mwasicho a sewing machine but the disputes which continued saw Groceman retreating back to Tiwi, and later to Giriama, and back to America in 2010 (Stephen 22.10.18).

Conclusion

It has been observed in this chapter that 16th century Christianity on the coastal regions of Kenya was short-lived. Though the blame has always been associated with Islam, investigations reveal that due to the ignorance of others cultures, there had been suspicion and constant misjudgement of one another. Because of the Portuguese unethical behavior, and a lack of love, they failed to Christianize the East African Coast. In other words, a golden opportunity to convert the indigenous people on the coast was lost. As this chapter has demonstrated, the Portuguese, though professing Catholic Christianity, had no heart for mission. It took another 300 years for a indigenous people to hear the Gospel from those who really had the passion for mission. The early missionaries' thinking about Africans created tension between the missionaries and the natives. This was due to a dictator-like attitude, domination, and paternalism. However, it is clearly seen that the missionaries who had some impact were those who did not impose their Western culture, but extended God's love and generosity to the local people. There are good examples of European missionaries such as Malcolm Heartnail, Wayne Richard, Groceman and others. Sadly, some of the indigenous converts were there for their own interest and gain. They did not necessarily feel the calling to evangelize the people. The contribution of Rev. John Krapf and his colleagues cannot go without adequate recognition, for indeed, the early translation of the New Testament in Swahili was a major contribution.

Chapter 4

Pioneer Digo-Duruma Christian Converts

By Japheth Muthoka

Introduction

In this chapter, I will discuss the earlier Christian Digo and Duruma converts in Digo land. The two communities live in Kwale County. The Digo community lives mainly along the coastal line while the Duruma community lives in the interior part of Kwale County, in what used to be called the Nyika area. The two sub-groups of the larger Mijikenda community have similar traditional beliefs and cultures. Commonly, they believe that the mother of the Durumas came from the Digo sub-group. The story goes further and says that two brothers (Mrima and Joto) who were Durumas, were given a job to graze cattle by a Digo man who later gave them his daughters as wives. To that extent, the difference between the Digos and the Durumas is the way they respectively pronounce words, hence different dialects in what is seemingly one language.

The Digo Community

Of importance to note is that the Digo are an East African tribe, concentrated on the southern coastal strip of Kenya between Mombasa and the border with Tanzania. It is rather surprising to find that in a country that is largely Christian, the Digo are nearly all Muslim. Needless to say, the Digo are a Bantu linguistic community; and are actually grouped together with eight other tribes. Together these sub-ethnic groups make up the Mijikenda, or "nine towns." Tradition tells us that the nine Mijikenda tribes originated farther north, but were driven south as a result of war.

It is also necessary to learn from history, especially about the great famine of 1899, and others before it, which resulted in them giving either themselves or their children as *kore* or 'blood money.' This was meant to serve as temporary collateral for a loan of food. There were times when the loan could not be repaid and so some were enslaved for this. Some earned their freedom after being taken to Mombasa where they were freed after converting to the creditors' religion (Joshuah 2018). Certainly, there were setbacks that need further critical examination.

Social and Economic Activities

Of importance to note is that the Digo people have from ancient times lived in fortified villages that consisted of 40 huts in each settlement. Due to their architectural designs, a person could tell who lived in which hut. For instance, while elders lived in round huts, other people lived in rectangular huts. Such strong loyalties to their cultural practices complicated the CMS attempts at winning the Digos to Christianity. Islam however was in another league as there had been trading with Muslim Arabs for many years. As a result, the pre-Christian East African coast saw the Digo people enjoying higher standards of living than most of their neighboring communities. They would trade with manioc, their principal crop. Manioc (Cassava) is a small shrub with thick roots that are eaten like potatoes. They would also grow sesame, corn, rice, beans; as 'palm wine' remained their revered drink (Joshuah 2018). In such a scenario, among other noted factors, the Christian mission in Digo land had a huge task in its bid to overturn the status quo. In the Christian mission, a campaign to encourage the Digo people to reassess some of their cultural practices that are not in tandem with the needs of our times is clearly necessary. A series of such workshops and conferences will be necessary at this moment in time.

Beliefs and Practices

Islam is more widely accepted among the Digo than among any of the other Mijikenda tribes. Nevertheless, ties with traditional practices (such as animism and ancestor worship) still have more influence on the Digo community than does Islam. Animism is the belief that non-human objects have spirits (Joshuah 2018). Ancestor worship is the practice of praying to deceased ancestors for help and guidance. One example of spiritism is their use of blood sacrifices. Such sacrifices are very significant to the Digo, especially in the exorcism of evil spirits. Witchdoctors are also consulted regularly (Joshuah 2018).

The Duruma Community

The Duruma people live on the semi-arid plains, one mountain range inland from the seacoast of eastern Kenya. The large city of Mombasa is the closest place where the Durumas may interact with other peoples. They are a mostly self-sufficient farming group with certain members becoming active traders with the outside world. All homesteads are members of one of 14 clans. Clan membership is determined by birth and not subject to change; the bride joins the husband's clan if it differs from hers. Marriage within homesteads is discouraged but most marriages are within the 14 clans (Joshuah 2018). Each family unit is affiliated with one of the 14 clans. Males take care of their families and they control the farming. Males also hunt wild animals and herd their domestic animals (i.e. cattle, sheep, goats, and chickens). Boys help with this. Women do all the household work assisted by the girls and also do a great deal of the farming.

Land is owned by the clan, not by individuals. The sons inherit land from their fathers including any goods or money they may have. Daughters do not receive any part of the inheritance.

Visitors can be initiated into one of the 14 clans of their own choice if they pay a subscribed fee to the panel of elders of that clan (normally a goat and a gourd of liquor, which is equivalent to 20 liters). Such a visitor is even entitled to the land of that clan, and can even use the names of that clan in his family. But for the land he is given, he is not supposed to plant permanent crops like coconuts, cashews, mangoes, citrus fruits and the like. After staying for a period of twenty years or more, such a visitor can be considered one of the clansmen, but it will depend on the extent of his respect and how he has lived peacefully with the clansmen who invited him. The population of Duruma now stands approximately at 491, 000, they are 65% Christian and the growth of the Christian faith is estimated to be 24% (Joshuah 2018).

Entry of the First Missionaries in Digo Land

The first European Christian missionaries in Digo land were Roman Catholics who came and did a survey from 1902 to 1904 and later settled in Waa in 1909. After finding resistance in Waa, the Holy Ghost Fathers who were the first white Christian Missionaries in Digo land, went to Kaloleni and set up a base at St. Georges Giriama and started evangelism there. Later in 1904, Rev. Bans and Rev. Binns of the Christian Missionary Society (CMS) from Kisauni, Mombasa, entered Waa and set up a base there. Then they moved to Matuga and later moved to Golini, then toTsimba, to Vyongwani, and finally to Zungu farm in Digo land in 1904. They later moved to Vitozani and Yapha in Duruma land (Kinango). In Vyongwani, they faced resistance; were beaten up, and two missionaries were killed and buried there together with their Bibles (Maneno 2018),

According to a source, Mzee Joseph Mwarsasiwa, an uncle to Canon Ramtu and Mzee Harry of Ganasani Village in Waa, was the first Digo Catholic Christian convert in 1909. Certainly, the Anglicans under Rev. Bans had a different mission with Zani, Mwagauchi, and others in 1904. This shows that the influence of the Roman Catholic white missionaries had begun to be felt soon after they settled in Waa. Joseph Mwarsasiwa later backslid and went back to becoming a Muslim; and was renamed Ali Harry. His two brothers Johana and Paulo also became Christian converts. Like Joseph Mwarsasiwa, Johana later became a Muslim. Paulo remained a Christian till his death. Among the challenges they faced was one where a Mosque was put up in their village of Ganasani at Waa. In its turn, the Mosque was used to complicate their work, and eventually flush them out.

Another early Christian Digo convert was Mr. Lugho Gore from Shamu in Ukunda later in 1910. He had to flee from Ukunda, to Jimba because of persecution with his family members and then to Frèretown-Kisauni, Mombasa, where he started a Church. The other earlier Christian converts' families from Digo land were the Ramtu family, the Zani family, the Maneno family, and the Mwalonya family, though they were largely Protestants. Mr. Mwalonya and Stephen Zani were schoolmates at Zungu farm in 1904, when later they converted to the Christian faith and were baptized by Rev. Bans (Maneno, 2018).

The Ramtu family married with the Zani family, while the Zani family married with the Maneno family and the Mwalonya family married with the Zani family. Among the members of these four Christian families were also Muslims. The members of these families have lived together and been more accommodating to one another and to the rest of society, especially when compared with their Muslim neighbors. Ven. Canon Elijah Ramtu who embraced the Christian faith in the early 1950s was chased out by one wing of his larger family who professed the Islamic faith in 1957. Ven. Canon Ramtu grew up in the Christian faith as a child. He later rose through ecclesiastical ranks to become the Diocesan Administrative Secretary and a Vicar General of Mombasa Anglican Diocese. At one time, he was the Provost of Mombasa Memorial Cathedral. By 2018, he was a retired, 83 year-old clergy men, but still active and participating in many of the evangelical works of the Christian mission in Digo land. Such duties included the translation of the Bible into the Digo language. Elijah Ramtu also participated actively in the book preparation for this volume.

Some of the other early Digo converts included Stephen Gude Zani, John Juma Maneno, and Nimrod Tabu from Vyongwani. They were first taken to Waa, where they were trained as carpenters. They were later taken from Waa to Kisauni, and then to Rabai for further training by the Church Missionary Society (CMS). They were baptized in Waa, between 1920 and 1923. Stephen Gude Zani later came back to Vyongwani and started a church at Vyongwani (now St. Stephens, ACK Church Vyongwani) in 1935. Stephen married Kerry Maboga. Mr. Maboga who was the father to John Juma Maneno, changed his name and called himself Maneno. Mr. Maboga had six children, four boys and two girls. Two of his male children, that is: John Juma Maneno (father to Samuel Maneno) and Thomas Mwakunena Maneno (father to Rev. Pore Maneno) became Christians. Two of his other male children,

Mwamaneno Maboga and Mr. Mwakunalwa Maboga became Muslims. One of the female children (Kerry Maboga, also called Nimaneno) became a Christian and the other female child, N'Kunena Maboga became a Muslim (Maneno 2018).

In regard to John Juma Maneno, he sired 10 children; and they all became Christians. This is mainly because all his children were born in Huruma, Nairobi (a Christian environment) when he was working in Kenyatta Hospital. Mr. Thomas Mwakunena Maneno had 7 children, 2 girls and 5 boys. Among the 7 children, only one (Rev. Simeon Pore Maneno) converted to Christianity, in 1957. The others became Muslims, though their father and mother were both Christians. Rev. Pore Maneno confesses that his decision to become a Christian was through parental encouragement (Thomas Mwakunena Maneno and Mercy Mtenga Chivumba). Mr. Stephen Gude Zani and his wife Kerry, John Juma Maneno and his wife Mary Chidzuga also encouraged him to go to church and they frequently used to offer prayers together at their respective homes.

Rev. Pore Maneno has 4 surviving children (Mercy Mtengo Maneno, Justus Baraka Maneno, John Johana Nasoro Maneno, and Emmanuel Pore Maneno). In 2018, all the siblings were confessing the God of Christendom. As noted earlier, the Digo community has mainly embraced the Islamic faith because it does not appear to contradict some of the ancient elements of African culture and tradition which they have been practicing from time immemorial. For example the Islamic faith was not against marrying many wives, which was in line with the Digo and Duruma cultures. The Christian faith insists on 'one-man-one wife' and not on 'one man, many wives.' However the Durumas have been more accommodating towards the Christian faith than the Digo communities, who have mainly embraced Islam.

Conclusion and Way Forward

In view of the previous information, the future of Christian evangelism and mission in Digo land lies in establishing institutions of social change with a strong Christian background, which will also have a positive impact on their social lives. It will therefore require further establishing of schools, hospitals, Bible schools, and other relevant institutions of higher learning with a Christian bias. A strategy geared towards reaching the Digo community for the Christian faith should also be thought out and be implemented without waiting too long. There is a need for the Christian families living among the Muslim Digo families to interact with them socially, especially during wedding celebrations, burials, and in other seaonal festivities within the Muslim calendar. Christians should have a cordial relationship with their Muslim brothers, but continue standing firm in their Christian faith. Further, Christians should be role models as they live together with their Muslim brothers. The Digo Christians who are living outside Digo land, in towns like Mombasa, Nairobi, and in the Diaspora, should support Christian evangelism in Digo land. Some of the ways to support Christian missions in Digo land will include training and ordaining more priests among the indigenous Digos. This can be followed by promoting them as Priests-in-charge of particular parishes within Digo land churches. Another approach would be to organize celebrations to mark critical events of Christianity in Digo land. The planned 100 years plus celebration of December 2018 is one of the ways of spreading Christian evangelism in Digo land.

The Duruma community has embraced Christianity and they have moved on to many other parts of Kwale County outside Kinango. Whenever they move to a new locality within Kwale County, they normally set up churches in the respective localities; and this is a commendable work as they always continue spreading the Christian faith. Indeed, the Duruma have moved to Lungalunga Sub-county, Matuga Sub-county, and a few of them have migrated to Msambweni Sub-county, in search of arable land for farming. This is because a large part of Kinango Sub-county experiences drought from time to time. Of importance to note is that the Christian Duruma community has always lived and co-existed cordially with their Muslim brothers. A good example of this co-existence is seen in the case of the Governor of Kwale, Salim Mgalla Mvurya, who is married to a Christian, Christine Mwaka, and living harmoniously despite belonging to their respective religious faiths.

Chapter 5

Christianity in Viongwani, Kwale County
Dr. Robert Maneno

Introduction

What is Christianity? Some say it is a religion, to others, Christianity is a means to an end, preying on the beliefs of others. All in all, Christianity is a monotheistic (belief that there is only one God) religion based on the life, death, resurrection and teachings of Jesus Christ. Over the last few centuries, Christianity and Christian ethics have played a prominent role in the shaping of Western civilization. During the early days of Christianity, communities were formed that would later be the pillars of modern day churches. They include; the Catholic Church, Protestantism, the Eastern Orthodox Church and Oriental Orthodoxy. In this chapter, the historical background of Christianity, the role of the families of Zani, Ramtu, Maneno, and Mawalonya and the voices of Muslims in Viongwani, will be briefly explored.

A Historical Background

In 1498, the first westerner from Portugal came to the shores of the Kenyan Coast, Vasco da Gama, and opened up Kenya and the entire East African community to the west (Wikipedia 2018). Afterwards, during the 18th century, missionaries like Johann Ludwig Krapf, Johannes Rebman, and David Livingstone, were among the first missionaries to come to Kenya and Tanganyika. They found heavy Islamic resistance from the Sultan of Oman and the locals who had converted to Islam. This did not stop them from carrying out their mission of preaching the gospel to the local population, and they established the first missionary church in Rabai Kilifi County in 1884. The church was founded as the diocese of Eastern Equatorial Africa (Uganda, Kenya, and Tanzania) with James Hannington as the first Bishop.

In 1904, the very first Church in Digo land was started in Zungu village. The pioneers of this church were Harry Kerr Binns, Anna Katherine, and Rev. Bans who were sent to Kenya by the Church Missionary Society. Another Church was also put up in Ziani village. Between the periods of 1904 to 1914, a significant number of locals were converted to Christianity. These locals included people like; John Mwarimo, Joseph Mwamwakoti (these two came from Chibuyuni village in the Golini area), Steven Gude Zani, Henry Bedzenga Madindima, Paulo Mwagasambi, the Ramtu family, and the Maneno family among others. Later, during the same period, Steven Gude Zani started his own church in Vyongwani village.

In 1914, the First World War unfolded, which saw countries like France, Russia, Italy, the United States of America, and the British Empire form an alliance to fight Germany and her allies. The British Empire included Great Britain and all its colonies which included countries like Kenya and Uganda among others. The war robbed both the allies and the central powers of their soldiers and thus a need for reinforcements occurred. The British turned to its colonies for men to fight in the war and women to work in its industries to support the war. This saw many African men transported to the West to help fight a war of which they were not a part (Wikipedia 2018).

Digo land was no exception. Many newly converted Digo Christians were selected and shipped off to join the war. Families were separated, fathers were taken away from their children, wives robbed of their husbands, young men taken away, all in the name of war. Things did not look good for the Africans who fought in the white man's army either, as they were subjected to racial segregation Some reports even indicate that they were often on the fore front of any battalion, as the "sacrificial lamb" one may say. They would sometimes be forced to carry heavy equipment through rough terrain and then be expected to fight. When the First World War began all the churches in Digo land collapsed except for two; Vyongwani and Matuga. Later, Matuga church also collapsed. Many Digos aspiring to convert to Christianity never converted due to a fear of being shipped off to the war.

There are some Digo men who were able to come back to their land after the war ended in 1918, one of these people was Mwalonya Lonya. Upon arrival in Digo land, he went back to the ways of the Digos. Eventually, he was baptized in the 1970s when he was already an old man. He later passed on in the year 1983 as a Christian.

The Holy Ghost Fathers, members of the congregation of the Holy Ghost and of the Immaculate Heart of Mary - A Roman Catholic Society of men founded in 1703 in Paris by Claude-Francois Poullart des Places, put up one of the first schools in Digo land known as Waa Catholic School in 1923, present day Waa Boys School (Wikipedia 2018). Back then, the missionaries taught technical skills like carpentry and masonry among other skills, to the local people. These skills empowered the local people and ensured that they could provide for their families.

Many local people joined Waa Catholic School. It was a place which was open to all people, and the missionaries did not discriminate against anyone. Among the local people who went to Waa Catholic School, four families played a major role in bringing Christianity to Digo land. These families include: The Zani family, the Ramtu family, the Maneno family, and the Mwalonya Lonya family.

The Roles of the Zani, Ramtu, Maneno, and Mwalonya Families

Steven Gude Zani was a very hardworking rice farmer who was married to Carolyn Tavikala Zani who came from the Maneno family. The name 'Tavikala' was due to the fact that Carolyn's parents kept losing children at birth, and they had lost hope of having any child until Carolyn was born. Together with his wife, they would harvest rice on their farm and used this rice to educate their children. Their children grew up to be successful people in society. They included; John Mahendo Masumbuko Zani: a councilor during the 60s and 70s on the Kwale County Council. With his two wives he had a number of children who were successful in life. Zacharia Zani, educated in Makerere, was a teacher, lecturer, and writer. He published the famous *Masomo ya Msingi*. He had prominent children including: Agnes Zani, a nominated Senator, Daniel Zani, a technician at the Ministry of Agriculture, and Onesmus Zani, a medical compounder (pharmacist) at Msambweni Hospital. Dick Zani received a Bachelor of Science degree at Makerere University and was later employed as the marketing manager at Bamburi Cement Factory. The daughters, who were also successful, included: Nelly Zani, Sophia Zani, Lizzy Zani, and Margaret Zani. Steven Gude Zani's greatest achievement was the church he started in Vyongwani as stated earlier.

The Ramtu family was comprised of two brothers, Joseph Ramtu and Mwahuruma Ramtu who settled in Waa.

Joseph Ramtu married the sister of Steven Gude Zani, Elizabeth Zani and together they were blessed with very dynamic children. The children included: Timothy Joseph Ramtu who was one of the Permanent Secretaries of the late President Jomo Kenyatta, Grace Joseph Ramtu, who was married to one of Mwalonya Lonya's relatives known as Shadrack Mwalonya Lonya, Naome Joseph Ramtu who was a nurse at Msambweni Hospital, Albert Joseph Ramtu who was an administrator at the East African Railways and Harbors, Nathaniel Joseph Ramtu, who was an accountant at the then Kwale County Council, Sammy Hatua Ramtu who studied in the USA, became a lecturer and married a sister to Tuva, and Mary Ramtu, the last born, who became a nurse, and then specialized in midwifery.

Mwahuruma Ramtu married and together with his wife had both Christian and Muslim children. They did not advance far with their education apart from Cannon Reverend Elijah Ramtu, who is still in active service. Mwahuruma's children included, Hamisi Mwagambere Mwahuruma, Jumaa Mwahuruma, Bakari Mwahuruma, Elijah Ramtu, Moses Mwahuruma (later changed by Islam to Saidi Mwahuruma), Leah Mwahuruma, Sarah Mwahuruma, Rachel Mwahuruma, and Christine Ramtu.

It is a very peculiar story about how the Maneno Family became Christian. It was during the burial ceremony of Chisinyo Maboga Maneno, the mother of Juma Maneno, when Juma Maneno miraculously was forced to go to the Waa School. How did this happen? As was the tradition of the Digos, whenever a senior or an elderly person died, the burial was usually accompanied by great celebrations of cultural dances and a lot of activities. John Juma Maneno, the son of Maboga Maneno and Chisinyo Maneno, was a tapper and he had broken his leg as he indulged in his daily tapping activities. The colonial Government at that time desperately wanted the locals to join the Waa Catholic School for an education. This was because fewer and fewer locals were showing up voluntarily to learn due to the factors mentioned previously (fear of being taken to war, even though the war was over). They had to use crude methods to get the locals to go to school. One of the methods was to send *askaris* (policemen) in plain clothes to snatch the young people from burial or wedding ceremonies, and then take them to school.

They used to wait until a time when people were really enjoying themselves to the fullest, then they made a signal to the other *askaris,* usually a whistle was blown, and then every *askari* got hold of as many young people as they could. John Juma Maneno was present at this ceremony together with his three brothers. Due to his injury, he was seated and was watching as the burial ceremony unfolded. So when the moment came, and people were having fun to the maximum, dancing and making merry, then all of a sudden, the whistle was blown. Everybody started running in different directions, because they knew well that the *askaris* were there to snatch the young people away, John Juma Maneno's brothers managed to run away, but unfortunately, or rather fortunately for him, due to his injury, he was unable to run; hence he was captured and was taken to the Waa Catholic School where he learned writing, mathematics, and reading, among other things. He learned carpentry and excelled. Within four years he had graduated. When he finished, he was posted to Msambweni Hospital where he worked for a short period. He went back to his home and returned to being a tapper because there was no other job and he had to take care of his family. He later received a letter from St. Johns Kaloleni Giryama to go and work as a carpenter. Due to his hard work and commitment he was later posted to King George the sixth Hospital, present-day Kenyatta National Hospital in Nairobi where he worked for 23 years.

While in Nairobi he became a strong Christian. While doing all these things, he also married his beloved wife - Mary Nkutawala Maneno, who came from the Muslim community. The Muslim community was not amused to see Mary Nkutawala married to the infidels or Christians. John Juma Maneno later developed ulcers because of the constant stress he had from his brothers - in-law. He retired in 1956 and returned home where he became a notable leader of the Shimba-Golini community. At one point or another, he was the school chairman of either Kwale Primary, Shimba Primary, Golini Primary, or Vyongwani Primary Schools. He was very active in the education of his people. During his free time he would go from homestead to homestead encouraging parents to take their children to school or else he would report them to the then District Officer, or the area Chief. He also was a pioneer when it came to constructing the road that leads from the tarmac road all the way to his home area in Vyongwani. He initiated a water project in Vyongwani which is still on-going. He and his wife were very active farmers. He started educating his children while he was still in Nairobi. Samuel Maneno attended Pumwani Primary School, and later joined Shimo La Tewa Secondary School. He then proceeded to Nairobi University and got his degree. He was once the Principal of Alliance High School and Lenana High School, among others. He also became the chairman of Kenya Ports Authority.

Other children of Juma Maneno included Winnie Maneno, Margaret John Maneno, and Dr. James Maboga Maneno, a medical doctor who got his degree at Makerere University. He was once Assistant Director of Medical Services and also worked with Unicef and Pathfinder among other organizations. Then came Robert Maneno, who did a number of courses. He first got his certificate in agriculture, and was posted to Kwale District, now Kwale County. Then he trained as a primary school teacher. After a while, he trained as a teacher for children with special needs, worked at Kwale School for the Deaf, then was posted to Coast General Hospital at the Speech and Hearing Department. While at Coast General Hospital, he proceeded to Finland where he got his advanced diploma and first degree in Special Needs Education. He was then called to teach at the Kenya Institute of Special Education from where he proceeded to Leeds University for his Masters degree in Speech Sciences. Robert Maneno did work as a Digo language project leader in Kwale County, where he initiated translation of the Bible into Digo, and also a literacy program in the Digo language. Currently, he is a lecturer at Pwani University.

Then came Joshua Maneno, who studied at Alliance High School, Nairobi University where he worked in geology. He received a Masters in Geology at Leicester University, and now he is a lecturer at Technical University of Mombasa. Simeon Maneno also did his high school at Alliance High School and got his first degree in Bio-Chemistry at Nairobi University. He received his Masters at New-Castle-Upon-Tyne in England. Simeon has worked as a health and safety officer in the coastal region to date. The young sisters include: Patience Ndombi, a lecturer at Nairobi Technical School, and Alice Maneno, a secondary school teacher in Migori.

Mwalonya Lonya was baptized in the 1970s and together with his wife had Joseph Mwachakurya Mwalonya. Joseph later left Christianity because he wanted to marry a second wife. His young brother David Pitu Mwalonya became a Christian, but married two wives, one was a Muslim and the other was a Christian. The Muslim wife had Muslim children while the Christian wife had Christian children, but all the children except one converted to Islam. Then came Paulo Nzala Mwalonya, who had two wives, a Christian wife and a Muslim wife as well.

Christianity played a major role in the development of the converted Digo families as indicated in the families mentioned above. Their living standards were better than the other locals who were reluctant to convert. The community believes that the right religion for Digos is Islam, and any one in any other religion is an infidel. A number of Digos who converted to Christianity had to revert back to Islam because they were never allowed to mingle with their immediate family members.

The Voices of Digo Muslims Concerning Christianity in Digo Land

Christians in Kwale County are only a drop in the ocean. I collected some views among some Digo Muslims. One of the respondents that seem not to see religious commonality between Christianity and Islam says;

Mimi nilikuzwa katika mazingara ya Kiislamu, kwa hivyo nikaonelea nieendelee hivyo hivyo kama vile wazazi wangu walivyokuwa. Kulingana na mimi hakuna dini mbaya, kwa sababu sote twamuomba mungu huyo mmoja.

I was socially brought up in a Muslim environment, therefore, I decided to follow the life of my parents. According to me, there is no religion that is evil because all of us worship the same God.

Criticizing some of the Christian funerary values, the same respondent claimed that,

Wakristo wanawatunza sana watu wao wakifa kwa kuwavisha nguo na kuwatengenezea majeneza mazuri. Kulingana na mimi hii si sawa na ni ku poteza tu pesa na kufanya mambo ambayo siya haki kwa Mungu. Waiislamu hawataki watu waliyokufa kuhifadhiwa kwa siku kadhaa. Kwa kawaida hupenda mtu azikwe punde tu anapokufa. Nashangaa sana kwanini wakristo wanawake wanakubaliwa kwenda kaburini kuzika?

Christians treat their dead relatives so well by dressing the dead and laying them down in good coffins. According to me, this is not economically good as it results in loss of money and practicing injustice before God. Musims do not desire to see the dead being preserved for long before they are buried. Normally, Muslims prefer a dead person to be buried as soon as they die. I have always wondered, why are women permitted to be present at the grave during burials?

He further categorically pointed out the mistakes that he thought were associated with Christian rites of worship saying:

Pia, naona si sawa kwa mtu yoyote kula mnyama bila kuchinjwa. Mimi kama muislamu na waislamu wengine nashangaa kwanini wakristo wanaenda katika nyumba za kuabudu wakiwa wamevaa viatu vyao. Mtume Issa anayeitwa Yesu kwa wakristo alikuwa akivua viatu alipokuwa akienda kuabudu katika masinagogi. Haya yote niliyozungumza mimi na waislamu wengine tunaona ni makosa, lakini tuna shangaa kwa nini maisha yao ni bora na wameendelea kuliko sisi waislamu.

Also, I think it is not proper for people to consume meat of an animal that has not been slaughtered. I and other fellow Muslims wonder, why do Christians enter houses of worship while wearing their shoes? Prophet Issa who is alo called Jesus by Christians used to remove his shoes whenever he entered the synagogues to worship. All that I have narrated here, I and other Muslims, regard to be bad practices, but we wonder why their [Christians] life is better and they are more socially and economically developed than us, Muslims.

A second respondent had this to say regarding his conception of the interplay between Islam and Christianity in shaping his family and personal identity and ethos:

Mimi babangu alikuwa ni mkristo na mamangu ni muislamu, Lakini baadaye, baba alibadilika akawa muislamu kwa sababu mama hakupenda Ukristo, na alikuwa yuko tayari kumuacha baba kwa sababu hiyo. Kwa hivyo baba akaona niheri awe muislamu ili aweze kuwa na mukewe. Mimi nilikuwa muislamu maana mama alikuwa muislamu. Na pia nilipenda sharia na kanuni za kiislamu hasa kuomba mara tano kwa siku. Pia nilipenda vile wanawake wakiislamu wanavyo vaa mavazi ya heshima. Mimi mwenyewe nina heshimu na naonelea hakuna dini mbaya. Nimegundua kwamba makanisa mengine hasa kule ninakoishi, hawapendi waislamu. Nao wanasema kwamba wale ambao si waislamu, nikama hawana dini. Pia sipendelei ukristo kwa sababu ya mavazi yao yasiyo kuwa na heshima.

My father was a Christian and my mother was a Muslim. But later my father changed and became a Muslim because my mother did not like Christianity, and she was ready to divorce my father for being a Christian. Therefore, my father decided to become a Muslim in order

> to preserve his marriage. In my case, I became a Muslim because my mother was a Muslim. I also admired the way Muslim women dress decently. I have my own honor and I presume there is religion that is bad. I have come to realize that some churches, especially where I reside, do not like Muslims. People there claim that those who are not Muslims, are like people who have no religion. I also do not like Christianity because they dress indecently.

Furthermore, the second respondent criticized the rejection of Western education by some Muslims. To this he commented:

> *Ijapokuwa waislamu wengi hawapendi elimu ya kisasa wanapenda madarassa, lakini mimi binafsi napenda elimu ya kisasa kwa sababu imeboresha maisha yangu na pia ya babangu. Baba ni muuguzi na mimi ni mwalimu na sasa naendelea na masomo yangu.*

> Although most of the Muslims prefer a Madrsassa to modern secular education, in my own case, I personally like secular education and even as I speak, I am currently persuing my education.

The third and last respondent also had this to say concerning his preference for Islam and his perception of the weaknesses of Christianity when compared to Islam in terms of worship, dress code, and scripture:

> *Mimi pia ni muislamu maana babangu alizaliwa muislamu. Vitu ambavyo sivielewi katika ukristo ni kwamba Yesu in mwana wa mungu. Hali sisi wailsamu tunajua kwamba yesu ni mtume wa mungu. Mimi kama muislamu na waislamu wengine tunashangaa kwa nini kuna biblia tofauti tofauti hali Quran iko vile vile tangu pale mwanzo ilipo andikwa haija geuka. Kitabu cha Barnabus hakiko katika biblia jambo ambalo lina nikanganya. Kulingana na mavazi ya kiislamu ninayapenda maana yake ya na heshma. Mimi napenda uislamu maanake ninaomba mungu moja kwa moja na bali sipitii kwa mtu*

yeyote kama wakristo wanavyo omba kupitia kwa Yesu Kristo.

I am also a Muslim because my father was born a Muslim. Some of the issues I do not understand in Christianity are things such as the claim that Jesus is a son of God. For us Muslims, we know that Jesus is God's prophet. I and other Muslims wonder why there are so many different types of Bibles yet the Qur'an has remained the same since it was written, it has not been translated. The book of Barnabas is not in the Bible, and this confuses me. Reagrding the Muslim dress code, I like it because it commands honor/respect. I like Islam because I worship one God directly without a mediator as Christians do by worshiping God through Jesus.

Conclusion

It had already been noted in this paper that while the emergence of Christianity was welcomed by certain members of the Digo community in Vyongwani, there was at the same time some resistance experienced from the Muslims. Both Christianity and Islam so far, seem to play a significant role in shaping the relationships among the Digo community in Vyongwani and Kwale at large.

Chapter 6

Anglican Church in Kwale County: A Brief History

By Peter Mwangi

The story of the Anglican Church and its existence can be traced back to 1904 as a result of evangelism done by the CMS missionaries from England. Currently however, the oldest existing Anglican Church center, which survived the onslaughts by anti-Christian forces, was established in 1914 and is found at Vyongwani. The CMS missionaries, Rev. Bans and Rev. Binns came to Kwale in 1904, secured a plot at Zungu, and subsequently fixed their beacons as a measure to isolate their plot from the rest. They then built a church, but after the First World War (1914-18), it was burned down. Debris and/or remains are still visible today (2018), and are a clear mark of remembrance. Kwale Tumaini Academy is currently built on the so-called Zungu plot.

The other church centers that were established were Mwachinga, Yapha, Vyongwani, Vuga, Marere, and Vitosani. Out of all these centers, only Vyongwani survived, and was being led by Mzee Stephen Zani who was a Catechist/Evangelist after he left Kisauni. After the students were taken to war in 1914, Stephen Zani went to Kisauni and started teaching there. He was in the process of being made an Anglican Deacon, but this did not come to be. He later returned to Digo land and went ahead with his catechism classes at Vyongwani center, which is now ACK St Stephens Vyongwani (Zani 1983). In my well-considered view, the major reason for the fall of the CMS Centres which had been established by 1915, was the start of the First World War (1914-18). During this difficult moment for the Digo mission, catechism and ordinary school students were taken to Ceylon, Burma, India, and other corners of the world to fight the "enemies" of the British Empire, despite this being a European crisis. When they returned, for those who did not die in the course of the war, they were hesitant to return to their catechism classes and/or school life. After all, they had already graduated in the broader sense of life abroad! Secondly, their spiritual bed had already been distrubed by Islam, which already dominated the area. Thirdly, the traditional religion had strongly regained prominence and consumed the spoils with impunity. To regain their lost territories, Zani and his Christian team had to work extra hard.

The Remnant Families

By remnant families, I refer to the famous four families that insisted that the Gospel was the way to go, irrespective of threats or death itself. That is, the Ramtu family, the Zani family, the Maneno family, and the Mwalonya family, who readily accepted Christianity and eventually joined the CMS missionary schools. A case in point is the Ramtu family, which was based at Waa. This is where the current Waa Boys High School is situated today. During those days, the church services were conducted at the Waa Primary School. In turn, Joseph Ramtu led the Ramtu family and other adherents of the Christian faith. In the 1950s, European settlers came and settled in the Shimba hills and started a church in 1952. The late Rev. Nimrod Mboje, a Taita man, relocated from Taita to Shimba Hills in the 1970s, and eventually became the first clergyman and was ministering to all the churches within Kwale County from Lunga Lunga to Taru. St. Matthias Shimba Hills, where Mboje was buried upon his death, became the headquarters of the Church; and all operations in the vast area came from this location. Additionally, the residence of the priest was also at Shimba Hills. Due to the long distances to the interior, it was very difficult for Rev. Mboje to walk to meeting places, hence most churches were established along the road for easy access. Without a vehicle or motorcycle, Rev. Mboje's passionate church ministry risked evaporating away in the hot lands of the East African coast. Nevertheless, Mgombezi Church was established in 1969 (Ramtu 2018).

Great Achievements Later!

In spite of Mwagauchi leaving the Zungu pioneer CMS missionary site out of fear for the consequences for burning Rev. Bans' school, church, and house, the church planting harvest boom followed later. Did the fire confirm that truly, "there is God in heaven"? Although Rev. Bans' trusted and leading student (Mwagauchi) did not burn the area intentionally, the fire was destructive in ways that were not normally like the biblical "burning bush" in Exodus 3 where Moses saw a strange fire that was not really burning up as fire normally does. In the case of Mwagauchi, he panicked and disappeared from the community. No one knows where he went, after his brothers (who were not converted) reminded him about slavery, capture, and other possible consequences. They scared him, and he lost faith in the Digo mission, just like his teacher Rev. Bans. But why fear? Moses didn't fear. He went closer, but was reminded to keep some distance, "take off your sandals, for the place where you are standing is holy ground" (Exodus 3:5). Afterwards, he was promoted and ordained for leadership. Mwagauchi and Rev. Bans would hear none of this. Clearly, God has many ways of communicating to the Digo mission or any mission for that matter. In the case of the Digo mission, great successes is what the fire signaled. It was a prophetic insight that showed that even though the building could be destroyed by fire or by anti-Christian forces, the success for the church ahead was immeasurable.

A case in point is the year 1914 when the church planting breeze under a new CMS priest, Rev. George Wright, came into vogue. Undoubtedly, he built churches in Vuga, Vyongwani, Golini Ziwani, Mwachinga, and Yapha. As noted earlier, the First World War aftermath left only Vyongwani, but with Stephen Gunde Nzani as the Lay Reader and Evangelist right from its establishment (Mwalonya 2018). Pangani church was started in early 1940s and was started by Mzee Charles and Benjamin Biro. The services at the Waa church were first performed in classrooms during the 1950s. This was after the fall of the church in Matuga (Mwalonya 2018). Such "fires" as in Exodus 3 signified and prophesied greater achievements to come.

Anglican Churches Within Kwale County

Shimba Hills Parish was started in 1952 and is the Archdeaconry headquarters. It was headed by Ven. Cpt. Nelson Mwanjala in 2018. It has one daughter church, namely Majimboni founded in 2018. By 2018, **Lunga Lunga Parish** was headed by Rev. Wellington Goja. It had two daughter churches namely: Mgombezi and Pangani. In turn, **Taru Parish**, started in 1974, was headed by Rev. Jairus Timeaus Munga in 2018. It was also the Parish headquarters. It had three daughter churches; namely, Samburu, Mghalani, and Chamamba (Munga 2018). Likewise, **Kinango Parish**, started in 1979, known as Emmanuel Kinango by 2018, served as the Parish headquarters. It was headed by Rev. Francis Kesi and had three daughter churches; namely, Bishop Hannington Miatsani, Bishop Kalu Chonyi, and Mabamani (Kesi 2018).

Kwale Parish was started in 1984, but the church at Vyongwani had been in existence since 1914. It was headed by Rev. Peter Mwangi in 2018, and had one daughter church, St. Stephens Vyongwani. Likewise, **Likoni Parish** started as an ACK guest house and later moved to its present site, where it was headed by Rev. Liston Okello by 2018. It had one daughter church, Waa - which is also a sub-parish headed by Rev. Julius Makame. In the case of **Msambweni Parish**, it was started in 2002 and was headed by Rev. Nelson Ndoro in 2018. It had one daughter church, Ghazi. As regards **Ukunda Parish**, it was started in 2002. By 2018, St. Paul's was its parish headquarters. Rev. Chrispus Ngowa was heading it by 2018. It had two daughter churches, Mwambungo and Mabokoni.

Concerning **Diani Parish**, it was started in 1984. St. Stephen Jadini was the parish headquarters and was led by Rev. Isaac Mwadziwe. It had one daughter church, Annabelle Kila Kitu. Similarly, **Mwaluvanga Parish** was started in 2014 and was led by Rev. Joshua Mwambi and had one daughter church, Kidiani. **Mwangwei Parish** was started in 2014 and was led by Rev. Patrick Ndara and had 5 daughter churches; namely, Ramisi, Perani, Shimoni, Kikonde, and Safarani (Ndara 2018). **Mafisini parish** was started in 2012 and currently is under the leadership of Rev. Alphonce Dzombo and has two daughter churches, Mwambadari and Mivumoni. **St. Paul's Majengo Mapya Parish** was started in 2015 and was led By Rev. James Okinyi and had no daughter church by 2018. **Lukore Parish** was started in 2016 and was led by Rev. Christine Chengo. **St.**

Johns Mtongwe Parish was started in 2017 and was led by Rev. Bernard Mwangulu and had one daughter church, Kibaki Estate.

In regard to the number of Archdeaconries, Digo land has three Archdeaconries (Kwale County) and has three Rural Deaneries, Shimba Hills Archdeaconry led by Ven. Cpt. Nelson Mwanjala, Matuga Archdeaconry led by Ven. Dr. Bryson Samboja, and Mariakani Archdeaconry led by Ven. Charlotte Mangi. Concerning the Rural Deaneries, it all falls into three Deaneries: Msambweni Deanery led by Rev. Cpt. Nelson Ndoro, Likoni Deanery led by Rev. Peter Mwangi, and Jimba Deanery led by Rev. James Gunga. Of importance to note is that Mariakani Archdeaconry and Jimba Deanery are in Kilifi County, and not in Kwale County, where the Digo mission is largely associated; but due to church boundaries Taru Parish lies under Mariakani and Jimba but the churches are geographically in Kwale County.

It is critically important to appreciate that there were other churches apart from the Anglican Church (or its predecessor CMS) that existed within the Digo mission and Kwale County, and were also started as early as the late 1890s. The Methodist Church in Mazeras is a case in point. It, however, did not penetrate to the interior, especially in those early days, but now has scattered all over by 2018. The Roman Catholic Church, the African Instituted Churches, and the Pentecostals have also claimed their share of the Digo mission. This shows that the growth and spread of Christianity is very encouraging in this part of the world, since it has been attracting diverse denominations. As a result, there is the ongoing development of the Bible Translation and Literature (BTL). In turn, BTL was busy translating the Bible into the Digo and Duruma languages by 2018, and by July 2019, the translators were planning to have completed the whole Bible in the local language. By 2018, BTL in Kwale was giving free New Testament Digo Bibles to the Digo readers who wanted to read the Bible in their own Chidigo language.

Anglican Church in Kwale County in 2018

Matuga Archdeaconry- Ven. Dr. Bryson Samboja
- Kwale Parish (1984)- Rev. Peter Mwangi
  - St. Stephen's Vyongwani (founded in 1914)
- Kinango Parish (1979)- Rev. Francis Kesi
  - Bishop Hannington Miatsani
  - Bishop Kalu Chonyi
  - Mabamani
- Ukunda Parish (2002)- Rev. Chrispus Ngowa
  - Mwambingo
  - Mabokoni
- St. Philip's Likoni Parish
- St. John's Mtongwe Parish (2017)- Rev. Bernard Mwangulu
  - Kibaki Estate
- St. Paul's Majengo Mapya Parish (2015)- Rev. James Okinyi
- Diani Parish (1984)- Rev. Isaac Mwadziwe
  - St. Stephen Jadini
  - Annabelle Kila Kitu
- Waa Sub-Parish

Shimba Hills Archdeaconry- Ven. Cpt. Nelson Mwanjala
- Shimba Hills Parish (1952)- Ven. Cpt. Nelson Mwanjala
  - Majimboni
- Lunga Lunga Parish- Rev. Wellington Goja
- Mgombezi
- Pagani
- Mwaluvanga Parish (2014)- Rev. Joshua Mwambi
  - Kidiani
- Mafisini Parish (2012)- Rev. Alphonce Dzombo
  - Mwambadari
  - Mivumoni
- Lukore Parish (2016)- Rev. Christine Chengo
- Msambweni Parish (2002)- Rev. Nelson Ndoro
  - Ghazi

- Mwangwei Parish (2014)- Rev. Patrick Ndara
  - Ramisi
  - Perani

Shimoni
Kikonde
Safarani

Mariakani Archdeaconry- Ven. Carlotte Mangi (Kilifi County)
    Taru Parish (1974)- Rev. Jairus Timeaus Munga (Kwale County)
        Samburu
        Mghalani
        Chamamba

Rural Deaneries
    Msambweni Deanery- Rev. Capt. Nelson Ndoro
    Likoni Deanery- Rev. Peter Mwangi
    Jimba Deanery- Rev. James Gunga (Kilifi County)

Conclusion

This chapter has outlined the rich Anglican history in Digo land. Methodologically, we have gathered the materials through primary schools, an activity where we interviewed relevant people, listened to their stories, and eventually isolated a few facts. We were able to appreciate the critical role of Rev. Nimrod Mboje, who overcame all odds and served the area during the darkest moments in the Digo mission. Rev. Mboje would minister to all the churches within Kwale County from Lunga Lunga to Taru. The chapter has also appreciated the prophetic insights that were derived from the fire that burned the first CMS buildings in Digo land in 1913. That is, like the case of Exodus 3 where fire was burning without consuming, the spirit of the mission in Digo land was not consumed; rather, great ministerial achievements awaited the Digo mission. As the 21st century surges on, we all have become witnesses that "blessed are those who have not seen and yet have believed," as Jesus told Thomas in John 20:29. Hence we shall not need to touch the wounds in order to believe that great things do happen. In the nature of things, we thank the missionaries and their good work of propagating the Gospel in the Digo and Duruma lands and the current Bishop of Mombasa, Rt. Rev. Alphonce Baya (since 2017 -), for coming up with the idea of documenting the history of the mission of the Church. We must also celebrate the panel of researchers, interviewers, and interviewees, and indeed I thank the Diocesan Research Unit for assigning me to research on the topic dealing with the Anglican Church within Kwale County. This, I have done faithfully and with much needed humility.

Chapter 7

Christian-Muslim Relations in Digo Land: A Historical Perspective

By Evans Mwangi

Introduction

The majority of the Kenyan people are Christians, with Muslims making up about 11% of its population, mostly along the North Eastern parts, within the Coastal region, and in cities such as Mombasa. Muslims in Kenya largely live along the Coast, while the inland population is predominately Christian, except in places such as Mumias. Other faiths practiced in Kenya are African Traditional Religions, and Hinduism (https://en.wikipedia.org/wikiReligion_in_Kenya). Muslims and Christians have a long history of peaceful coexistence in Kenya. To this end, African hospitality is crucial to Christian-Muslim relations in Kenya, since it reminds their followers that they should love one another because of their African identity and philosophy first. In the Kenyan coastal towns of Mombasa and Lamu, Muslims and Christians live as neighbours, and they work together in response to local problems, such as drought, violence, and crime, hence creating an image of the "other" as people with whom one can work for a better communal life (Olando 2017:124).

On the Kenyan Coast, we have a reasonable number of Muslims found largely in the south coast, Kwale County. In this county, the

Digos and Durumas are the majority of people who live here. These two communities are among the nine coastal sub-ethnic groups, commonly known as *Miji Kenda*. Though there are Durumas who are Muslims, over 70% of the Digos are Muslims in this region. We still have Christians in this area, though few. In this chapter, I refer to Digo land as the entire Kwale County, which is essentially occupied by Digo and Duruma people.

The aim of this chapter is to trace the history of how Digos became Muslims. I will also give the history of the Digos who first converted to Christianity. I am going to attempt to explain historically how Christians and Muslims co-existed from 1904 to the present. African Traditional religion is important among the local inhabitants of Digo land especially among the Digo people. I am therefore going to show how it contributed to the conversion of Digos to Islam. Finally I will explain how the relationship between Christians and Muslims began and continues into the 21st century in Kwale, Digo land.

The Coming of Islam to Eastern Africa

Kenya is a country found in the eastern part of Africa. It has a coastline along the Indian Ocean. Consequently, for one to know how Muslims arrived in Digo land, which is situated along the Kenyan Coast, one will have to trace the history from the time the Muslims came to East Africa. The association between East Africa and Arabia can be traced back during the pre-Islamic time. History shows that Arab sailors were present in the second century AD and were moving between the Arabian Peninsula and the coasts of East Africa for business purposes. Their ships' movements would increase in calm seas and decrease when the tides were high; based on the directions of the monsoons. Additionally, the sources pointed out that different types of commercial activities had thrived among the two areas, including trade in ivory, fabrics, chewing gum, and animals. Arab traders were coming with cloth, food stuff, iron, weapons, and returning with ivory, frankincense, Arabian gum, animals, and other items (Al-Sayyar 1975).

At the early stages of the 7th century, Islam arrived on the coast of East Africa through some Arabs Muslims who immigrated to Africa for economic and political reasons. Some historical writings, which were found on the ruins of several mosques in Gede, Lamu, and Pate, date back 1000 years, and show the arrival of Arabs in the Kenyan coastal areas. They exercised trade activities through important routes from the Southern Arabian Peninsula and the Red Sea to the new settlements which they established along the coastal line (Al-Naqira 1986). Likewise, Archaeologists confirm a flourishing Muslim town on Manda Island by the 10th Century AD/CE. (Salim 1973). The Moroccan Muslim explorer, Ibn Battuta, visiting the Swahili Coast in 1331 AD/CE, told of a strong Muslim presence in Zeila, Mogadishu, Lamu, Malindi, and Mombasa. Ibn Battuta said: "The inhabitants were pious, honourable, upright, had well-built wooden mosques and belonged to Shfi'i school of Islamic Jurisprudence" (Ibn Battuta, 1987).

From this information, it is clear that there has been a presence of Muslims on the coast of East Africa for a long time. Although coastal rulers did not send missionaries into the interior, local Africans embraced Islam freely through attraction to the religious life of the Muslims. Close integration with the local population helped to foster good relations resulting in Islam gaining a few converts, based on individual efforts. Most of the surrounding Bantu communities had a close-knit religious heritage, requiring a strong force to penetrate. The pacification and consolidation by European powers provided the much-needed force to open up the communities for new structures of power and religious expression (Trimingham 1980:58).

Progress in the spread of Islam in Kenya came between 1880 and 1930. This was when most social structures and the African worldviews were shattered, leaving them requiring a new, wider worldview encompassing or addressing the changes experienced. Consequently, Islam introduced new religious values through external ceremonial and ritualistic expressions, some of which could be followed with no difficulty. Socio-culturally, Muslims presented themselves with a sense of pride and a feeling of superiority. Islamic civilization was identified with the Arab way of life (*Ustaarabu*), as opposed to "barbarianism" (*Ushenzi*) hence the domination of a form of Arabism over the local variety of Islam. As we shall see later, this is one of the many reasons as to why most people in Digo land were converted to Islam on the Kenyan coast.

Christianity on the Kenyan Coast

The arrival of Christianity in the Kenyan coast was seen when the Portuguese fleet under the command of Vasco da Gama anchored off Mombasa towards sunset on Saturday, April 7, 1498. This fleet had carried some priests on board ship who used to provide spiritual welfare for the crew. The Portuguese, who were devout Catholics, carried priests in all their fleets sailing to the far corners of the world to minister to the crews and to seek converts in the lands they visited. Several groups of Portuguese missionaries came to East Africa between 1500 AD/CE and 1700 AD/CE. In 1567 CE/AD, a group of Augustinian priests built a Monastery at Mombasa. Next we hear of Augustinian friars who built a church on Mombasa Island in 1598 at the site of the present day Old Customs House, and soon were claiming 600 converts from the local populace (Sparrow 2011: 17).

In 1607, a new Catholic mission society arrived in Mombasa. They were called the Brethren of Mercy, and their main work was caring for people who had been converted from Islam. By the end of the 17th century, the Portuguese began to lose their hold on East Africa. At the same time, Catholic missionary activity began to decline. By the beginning of the 19th century, there were no Roman Catholics left along the coast, except for some foreign traders (Sparrow 2011: 17). We later find Christian missionaries returning to Mombasa in 1844, when the Rev. Dr. Ludwig Krapf reached the East African Coast on behalf of the Anglican Church Missionary Society. He asked for permission from the Sultan of Zanzibar, and he and his wife went to work and live in Mombasa town. He failed to make any converts, and two years later, after the death of his wife and baby, he and a fellow missionary moved to the mainland and established a mission at Rabai Mpya, where the indigenous leaders had given him a friendly welcome. There, in 1848, Krapf opened the first Anglican Church in the territory that is now Kenya. On the mainland immediately adjacent to Mombasa Island, the CMS built Emmanuel Church in Frèretown, a settlement established in 1875 for liberated slaves (Sparrow 2011:18-19).

Introduction of the Muslim Religion

Digo people who live on the southern coast of Kenya as stated earlier, are largely Muslim, and at the same time practice African traditional religion. In my interview with Canon Elijah Ramtu, a retired priest with the Anglican Church of Kenya, Mombasa Diocese, on October 10, 2018, at Kwale town, he noted,

> Islam is widely accepted among the Digos but tied in with traditional practices, such as spiritism and ancestral veneration. Blood sacrifices are very important to the Digos, particularly in the exorcism of evil spirits and witchdoctors are also consulted frequently. Most Digo people only have a shallow understanding of Islam's principles and doctrines. Though they know no religious meaning for wearing the black veil, Digo women wear it to show respect for their husbands. (Ramtu 2018)

Islamic traders visited the coast of Africa as early as the 10th century and had contact with the Digos that they found on the East Coast of Africa. Many Digos converted to Islam in the 1920s. Arab traders who visited Digo land traded at Gasi, Shimoni, and Vanga. They were said to have come from Zanzibar in what was then Tanganyika, present-day Tanzania. Among the first Mosques built at this time, one was at Nganasani and another at Chinondo. It is therefore, most likely that the first Digos and Durumas to become Muslims were those who lived around these areas (Maneno 2018). Furthermore, looking at the way the Arabs were smart and clean in their white *kanzus*, Digos were attracted. Another important point to note about the spread of Islam in Digo land in the 20th century was Arabic culture, which allowed Muslims to practice witchcraft and polygamy. Already Digos were polygamous and their culture sanctioned black magic practices too. Since the Islamic religion did not prohibit the Digos from exercising their African traditional cultures and religious practices together with Islam, it was easy then for most Digos to accept the Islamic religion (Maneno 2018). Christians and Muslims in Digo land in Kenya have co-existed for a long time. So, like in other parts of the country, cases of Muslims' conversion to Christianity and Christians' conversion to Islam occurred frequently. Consequently, when you would take a walk in the afternoons and evenings at the shopping centers and market places in Kwale County, Muslim open air preaching (commonly known as *mihadhara*) was a common sight (Ramtu 2018).

Mihadhara is a plural of the Swahili word, *mhadhara* meaning a lecture, a public talk, or a discourse. The word has its origin in the Arabic root, *hadara*, which means "to be present" or "to present a lecture". Two Kiswahili words also show the meaning of the term, the verb *kuhudhuria* "to attend", and the noun *mhudhurio* "attendance". Therefore, when an issue is to be discussed publicly, it is conducted *'hadharani* (Wandera 2008:95). *Mihadhara* is nowadays not allowed by the Kenyan government after it was seen to be a threat to peace in areas where Christians and Muslims co-exist. However, according to Kiilu, a pastor in one of the Pentecostal churches in Digo land, *Mihadhara* still occurs, though at a lower profile at this place, but only between the Seventh Day Adventist Church and some Muslim Clerics (Kiilu 2018). Ramtu (2018), added that during *Mihadhara* time, Muslim preachers would read the Bible. Then after misinterpretation of the selected biblical verses, they would try to convince Christians to convert to Islam. Another method was to use the Muslim girls, who would ask Christian men to become Muslim first as a condition before getting married to them.

Introduction of Christianity

The first well known Digos in Kenya to become Christians were the Manenos, the Ramtus, and the Zanis. Others not so much known outside are the Mwalonyas and the Gakuryas. However, due to strong Islamic pressure which came later, the Gakuryas converted to Islam. Another man said to have become a Christian in those early years was Samuel Lugo Gore who is said to have fled away to the Kisauni area of Mombasa city, due to family disputes and fear of being attacked by Muslims because of converting to Christianity. On reaching Kisauni, he found Christians who were former slaves and joined them. It is said that he later trained to be a catechist and went to Jimba in Rabai. He founded Jimba Mission Center which is in Kilifi County. The Center is named after him, Canon Lugo Gore Mission. These first Digo Christians were not Muslims, not at any point in their lifetimes. They were followers of the African traditional religion. Islam had not reached Digo land by this time (Maneno 2018).

John Juma Maneno, later relocated after getting a job in Nairobi and settled there, and would only come back home during Christmas time. According to Samuel Maneno, son of John Maneno, 79, a retired teacher, the church at Vyongwani (their home area now at Kwale County) would open its doors during this time. The preacher would be John Juma Maneno and his family formed the congregation. After he left, the church would close its doors again until the next Christmas holiday (Maneno 2018).

On the other hand, Ramtu went to work at Kilindini Harbour in Mombasa Port. His children followed him and later some went to study in Nairobi City. Some studied at Alliance High School. Similarly, this family of Ramtu would be seen in Digo land during Christmas only. Christians and Muslims would celebrate Christmas together hence the evidence for their co-existence (Ramtu 2018).

Christian-Muslim Relations

Looking at the relationship between Christians and Muslims then, Matuga area was generally peaceful during religious festivals like Christmas and *Idd fitul*. Subsequently, the few Christians who remained behind suffered intolerance, as in the case of Canon Elijah Ramtu who held that he himself was seriously isolated by his cousins because he was the only Christian at home then. He explained to me how he was not allowed to study in school with the rest of the children who were principally Muslims (Ramtu 2018). Later on, the intolerance spewed over to the other few Christians who lived in the Matuga area. As a result, Muslims became rough with the few Digos who were Christians. Some of these early Christians would have their wives taken away because of not converting to Islam. Ramtu explained: "My cousin had his wife taken back by the in-laws until he would become a Muslim, just in case he wanted his wife back" (Ramtu 2018).

In the 21st century however, Christian-Muslim relations appear to be pleasant in Digo land. People from the two main faiths celebrate Christmas and *Idd fitir* together. Christians invite Muslims to celebrate Christmas together and Muslims, during Idd do the same and invite Christians to celebrate with them. In other ceremonies also, people attend weddings and burials together. This shows there is a cordial relationship despite different religious beliefs (Kiilu 2018). The peaceful atmosphere is also brought about by the presence of other people from the rest of Kenya. They have settled in the Kwale area now. This has forced both Muslims and Christians to learn peaceful co-existence or perish together. This has driven them to constantly hold interfaith meetings so as to discuss issues affecting their respective followers (Kiilu 2018).

However, the greatest enemy of peaceful co-existence among Muslims and Christians in Digo land is their profound adherence to their African culture and traditional religion. Samuel Maneno, in a phone interview on October 15th 2018 noted,

> The culture has gotten into the Digo people so much that it is almost difficult to change their ways of life. Even those who are Muslims, they are not so much into Islamic practices and beliefs as they are in to their traditional beliefs and practices. This, in my view, has been the main reason why it has become almost impossible to evangelize the Digos in particular. It is easier to preach to a Duruma than a Digo because of the deeply rooted nature of his African customs and practices. In addition, the Digos' strong adherence to their faith in the African culture has not only taken them far from the savior of the whole of humanity, but it has also brought poverty to their doorsteps in the Kwale County area. (Maneno 2018)

Conclusion

The aim of this chapter was to show the history of Islam and Christianity on the southern coast of Kenya, Kwale County since 1904 to the present and how the followers of the two faiths co-existed up to the present. The other reason was to stipulate how the African traditional religion contributed to the Digos becoming Muslims. I have managed to show that the Indian Ocean trade played a vital role in having early Muslim traders reach Digo land in the 1920s and helped convert many Digos to Islam. The first Arab-Muslim lifestyles, including dress, made it easy for the Digos to convert to Islam. The other factor that made the Digos become Muslim was the practices of the Muslim religion like those of marrying many wives and the practicing of witchcraft. These practices were similar to those of the Digo people, and so it was easy to follow Islam and at the same time remain rigid in their African practices. Christian-Muslim relationships at first appeared to be peaceful during religious festivities like Christmas and Idd. However, Christians were discriminated against even to the point of being threatened that their wives would be taken away if they did not become Muslims. As we have also seen, young Christian men who would want to marry were told to become Muslims first as a condition before marriage. Christians would not be allowed to attend the same schools as Muslims. There was intolerance in these schools. Presently, Christians and Muslims in Digo land co-exist peacefully. They attend ceremonies like weddings and burials together. Generally there seem to be cordial relationships now between the followers of the two faiths.

I have also shown that African traditional religion in Digo land is an enemy of the two religions and particularly Christianity, which does not allow syncretism. I have shown that the Digo are deeply rooted in their African customs, beliefs, and practices since time immemorial. For Christians to do effective mission and evangelism work in Digo land, serious evangelistic methods have to be employed. A thorough understanding of the Digo African customs and beliefs has to be done with the help of the few Digo and Duruma Christians. We Christians also have to devise innovative and effective methods of eradicating poverty in Digo land as this is another reason why numerous people have remained non-Christians.

Chapter 8

Unsung Heroes and Heroines in the Digo Mission

By Julius Gathogo

Introduction

Grammatically, unsung hero refers to a person who does great deeds but receives little or no recognition. Certainly, 114 years of the Digo mission (1904-2018) cannot lack critical people who are unfairly forgotten, ignored, and/or left out despite their gallant efforts to see to its success. Such are the men and women who run the engine of success, sometimes, without getting noticed. In a patriarchal society, women bear the worst brunt when their efforts aren't chronicled in the annals of history. Undoubtedly, when a society ignores its own heroes and heroines in the guise of "forward ever, backward never" and other subtle slogans, it eventually dies. An Africa that does not tell her own stories will always remain an appendage in other people's histories. Considering that there hasn't been a huge impact as in the case of Rabai mission, Mutira mission, Baganda mission, or even Weithaga mission, one may be tempted to ignore the little contributions so far made.

Considering that the population of Christians in the Digo dominated Kwale county of Kenya is below 2%, 114 years later, while Islam boasts of 79% as traditionalists claim 20%, one will easily view the Digo mission as a failed project that does not need our attention. Conversely, this should drive us to ask: What were/are the impediments to the Digo mission and what can we do about it in the 21st century? Considering that he who wears the shoe best knows where it pinches, we are the best placed people to explore the cure for the Digo mission. Apparently, an European missionary from the Church Missionary Society (CMS), Rev. Bans, announced his inability to continue with it after laboring for 8 years (1904-1912), and chose to move upcountry instead. Indeed, those who are in close proximity to the Digo mission should do much better than Rev. Bans. Undeniably, an Africa that does not tell her own stories will always remain an appendage in other peoples' histories.

Heroes and Heroines

In the Digo mission, both locals and "outsiders" played a critical role since 1844 when Ludwig Krapf introduced the modern Protestantism as we know it today. There are those who worked for the positive progression of Digo mission from "abroad" and there are locals in Digo land who were conversely working towards its destruction from within. Nevertheless, several names will always come up of people who either sought to launch Digo mission, reinforce it, or to resuscitate it from time to time. Rev. Canon Binns first travelled to Marere near Godoni forest of Digo land in 1878 and 1879 though no known contribution can be noted. Later, as the all-powerful Secretary of CMS and Archdeacon of the vast region where Digo land was a part, Rev. Binns' was active in the supply of relief food during the 1899 famine that hit the region. As the person who handled CMS monies, Rev. Binns was also instrumental in funding the activities of the founding clergy, Rev. Bans. Binns all-powerfulness is seen when he openly clashed with Bishop Alfred Tucker after he suspended a pioneer African clergy in their Kisauni Centre, Rev. Ishmael Semler, over the methodology in conducting of marriage ceremonies in the Anglican Church. As Semler stuck to the traditional Anglicanism in conducting marriage ceremonies, Binns turned more liberal, hence the source of their conflict. When Bishop Tucker told him to concentrate on his CMS position and leave transfers and suspensions of clergy to the Bishop, Rev. Binns stood his ground. In other words, his powerful position of CMS Secretary made him a major stakeholder for the CMS missions in the East Coast of Africa.

Equally important is the presiding Anglican Bishop since 1884 in the first Diocese of the Eastern Equatorial. The Bishops deserve a mention as heroes of the Digo mission because they had a direct and indirect role in the state of affairs. They include the first Bishop of Mauritius (Vincent W. Ryan) whose primacy began in 1862 and ended in 1872 when he retired. By then, the entire East and Central Africa was under Bishop Ryan (Gathogo 2013). Others are the first Bishop of Eastern Equatorial Africa (James Hannington) who reigned from 1884 to 1885; Henry Perrot Parker who served from 1886 to 1888; and the third and last Bishop of Equatorial Africa, Alfred Robert Tucker, who ministered from 1890 to 1897. By the time the Digo mission was official in 1904, the Bishop of Mombasa was William George Peel – who ministered from 1897 to 1916. After Rev. Bans surrendered and eventually abandoned the Digo mission, as he protested the difficulty in stewarding it in 1912, Bishop Peel still went on to post another clergy in his place. In other words, Bishop Peel still had faith in the success of the Digo mission.

Further succeeding bishops of Mombasa had a critical role too, despite the fact that they are not yet celebrated for their attempts at reshaping the Digo mission. They include: Richard Stanley Heywood who served as the second Bishop of Mombasa from 1918 to 1936; Reginald Percy Crabbe who served as the third Bishop of Mombasa Diocese from 1936 to 1953; Leonard Beecher who served as the fourth Bishop of Mombasa (1953-1960) and as the first Archbishop of East Africa (1960-1970); and Peter Mwang'ombe who served as Mombasa Diocesan Bishop from 1964 to 1979. Peter Mwang'ombe was educated at St. Paul's United Theological College, now St. Paul's University, Limuru, and ordained as a priest in 1945. He was the Archdeacon of Mombasa from 1955 to 1964. He remains an unsung hero in the Digo mission for several factors. First, his interest in the Digo mission came out clearly when he ordained the first indigenous clergy from Digo land, Elijah Kubeta Mwahuruma Ramtu (1936-), in 1975.

The sixth Bishop of Mombasa Anglican Diocese was Crispus Dolton Nzano. Nzano's importance in the Digo mission is seen in the fact that he liaisoned with the Teachers Service Commission to train the second indigenous clergy, Simeon Pore Maneno (1949-), at the present day St. Paul's University, Limuru, from 1982 to 1984, after which he made him an Anglican Deacon and later ordained him in 1985. Further, in posting Rev. Maneno as Chaplain, and a missionary of the vast Kwale County, dominated by the Digo and Duruma ethnic groups, the Bishop clearly demonstrated his concern. The seventh Bishop of the Anglican Diocese of Mombasa, Julius Robert Katoi Kalu, whose episcopacy lasted from 1994 to 2017, also showed great interest in the Digo mission. His appointing of Ven. Canon Elijah Kubeta Mwahuruma Ramtu, a Digo by ethnic extraction, as his de-facto number two (Vicar General) was an encouraging step. Was he hoping to attract the Digo people to the Anglican Christianity via this appointment? Certainly, Ramtu as a person has always been described as one of the most competent clergy in the entire Anglican Communion in Kenya. Kalu also commissioned Ven. Dr. Bryson Samboja as a missionary in Digo land since 2007. Additionally, Kalu ordained the first indigenous Digo woman clergy, Rev. Evylene Asha Manjewa in 2009; and Rev. Grace Ruvuno Rehema, also from Digo land, was ordained in 2011. In 2002, Bishop Kalu ordained Rev Rhoda Ruvuno Wabukala who was serving among the Digo. The eighth Bishop of Mombasa since 1884 is Alphonce Mwaro Baya, whose interest in the Digo mission was seen clearly after he formed the Diocesan Research Unit (DRU) in mid-2018. Interestingly, he requested the members of the DRU to prioritize their research on Digo mission and complete a well-researched book on Digo mission by mid December 2018. Baya has also been the Vice Secretary of Global Teams, an association which works in Kwale to promote the holistic welfare of the Digo.

While the concern in this chapter is the African contribution to the Digo mission, who served under hostile environments where they were/are largely seen as traitors, we must appreciate the role of two pioneer CMS missionaries, Revds Binns and Bans. In particular, Rev. Canon Harry Kerr Binns (1852-1935) played a critical role, though his works are not easily seen as he never served as the resident priest of the area. Nevertheless, his role as the CMS Secretary since 1899 and Archdeacon of the vast area of the entire coastal region till he retired in 1923 and returned to live in Somerset, England, cannot be gainsaid (Binns, 2018). In controlling the office that had the resources, he contributed heavily through Rev. Bans who officially founded the Digo mission in 1904. Although Rev. Bans was overwhelmed by the "difficulties" in the Digo mission after barely 8 years, Rev Binns and the serving Bishop William Peel were able to send missionaries to Digo land later, hence the reason the mission exists to date. It is imperative to address his pedigree and other factors within his formative years as a European missionary to Africa.

Rev. Canon Harry Kerr Binns (1852-1935)

Born in 1852, in the United Kingdom, Harry Binns began his public life as a painter in a Porcelain factory. At barely 19, he was already a clerk in Worcester, UK. After completing his theological education at Church Missionary College in 1875, he was made an Anglican Deacon. Subsequently, he served as a curate in Whittingham, Worcestshire. On March 19, 1878, he was ordained as an Anglican priest by the Archbishop of Canterbury at Croydon Parish Church. He was subsequently commissioned as a missionary and/or the priest to the colonies.

Rev. Binns' first contact with the Digo mission was in 1878 and 1879. Like a surveying missionary, he visited Jilore, a settlement in Kenya's Kilifi County, near Malindi, and the Godoni forest area, Marere of Kwale County. Although, the first European missionary in the Digo mission is normally reported to be Rev. Bans, it is worthwhile to concede that Rev. Binns was there before 1904, even though his missionary activities then were not public. In fact, some sources simply say that he visited Jilore (Kilifi county) and Godoma (Kwale county) (see Binns, 2018). Was the name Godoni misspelt and finally put as Godoma? Or have the names changed? Nevertheless, the present day name in Kwale County, is Godoni where there is a forest. While my interviews in the field had issues with the name, Godoma in Kwale County, where Rev. Binns visited in 1878 and 1879, does exist in Kwale county of Kenya. In fact, Godoma is cited as one of the more populous areas in Kwale County in the 21st century. Other populous areas include: Kikoneni, Mabafweni, Mangawani, Lukore, Mwananyamala, Mwandeo, and Mamba (Geoview 2018).

According to Rev. Binns diary, which appears on the web, he was a missionary at Feretown from 1882 to 1883. With time, Freretown replaced Leven House (on Mombasa Island) as the centre for English missionaries. It is not clear where Rev. Binns was from 1880 to 1881, though it is possible that he returned to the UK after surveying the Rabai and Digo missions; and only returned in 1882 as an organized operator. In February 1884, Rev. Binns was an immigrant to Victoria,

Australia aboard the *Rosetta*. He was accompanied by a Black African (the so-called Bombay Africans) from Kisauni and India, his wife, and an infant. It is from there that he became a curate in Perth, Tasmania an island state of Australia. Geographically, this is located 240 kilometres to the south of the Australian mainland, which is separated by the Bass Strait. Before docking back on the East African coast in 1899, he served a curate in Bradley, Worcs (1888); and at St. James, Tauton, Somerset. It is in 1889 that he was appointed as the Secretary of the Church Missionary Society, for the East African mission (Binns 2018). Although the *Daily News* newspaper, founded by Charles Dickens as its first editor in 1846, reported on October 4, 1892 that Rev. Binns had been in Freretown, Kisauni, where the Digo mission was located and where he had first operated, his diary is silent about this. Additionally, a brief history of Emmanuel Church, Kisauni, Freretown, on their church website, shows that Rev. Binns served this church, on the East African coast, from January 10, 1876 to April 2, 1922 (Kisauni 2018). He was apparently a roving pastor who was travelling to Australia and back to the East African Coast.

While operating from Kisauni, Freretown, mission headquarters, which was gradually replacing Leven House on the Mombasa Island, Rev. Binns ecclesiological activities are clearly visible. For instance, *The Times* newspaper had reported, on December 22, 1896, that he had presided over a marriage ceremony in Freretown, Mombasa. On February 4, 1899, the *North Wales Chronicle* newspaper had also reported on severe starvation in the entire East African coastal region where Rev. Binns, as CMS Secretary, responded appropriately with relief food (Binns 2018). Starvation also hit areas covered by the Digo mission (Kwale, Matuga, Lungalunga, and Msambweni). In 1923, Rev. Canon Binns retired as the Archdeacon of the vast area that covered the East African coast (then called the Mombasa Archdeaconry), and returned to Somerset, UK, where he revised and re-arranged the Swahili-English dictionary of the pioneer CMS missionary, the Rev. Dr. Ludwig Krapf, which he completed in 1925 (Binns 2018). Despite his death on February 22, 1935 at Pen Selwood, Bourton, Dorset, in the United Kingdom, his imprint remains fresh on the Digo mission, 83 years later (1935-2018). He died at 83 years of age.

Rev. Bans

Unlike Rev. Binns, whose diary has been partly posted by his family, and which also appears in some published works, Rev. Bans' history disappears from the public record the moment he abandoned the Digo mission in 1912. As he quit the Digo mission, he complained that it was too difficult for him from all angles (Zani 1983). As the Digo people stuck to their traditional religion and Islam, which had dominated the area, Rev. Bans could not see the future of the Christian mission in Digo land despite his gallant efforts. Worst of all, his adherence to a Christological methodology in the mission with a 3-fold ministry did not work (Zani 1983). That is, he evangelized (through building of a make-shift church), taught (through establishing a school in Digo land), and healed (through establishing a dispensary to provide first aid). Yet this did not yield the satisfactory fruits Rev. Bans had envisaged, thus he left the mission after barely 8 years in the field.

Evangelist/catechist Stephen Gude Zani (1899-1985) saw Bans in 1904 when he came to establish the Digo mission (Zani 1983). The three African assistants who accompanied him, namely: Macheche Baraka from Rabai, Njuguna, and Munuhe Munene who equally must also be treated as unsung heroes. Their actual names cannot be spelt out clearly, nor can we tell their first names, but their impact remains, 114 years later (1904-2018). Another unsung hero in the initial stages of the mission is Mwagauchi, an indigenous person from Digo land. According to evangelist Stephen Zani (1983), who was an eye-witness, Mwagauchi was the only one who remained after Rev. Bans left. From Rev. Bans, he had learned new forms of farming, reading and arithmetic, Western medicine, and basic bibliology. Mwagauchi also learnt about good stewardship of resources and time; hence the reason why he faithfully took good care of the buildings and other resources that Rev. Bans had left behind. However he encountered a misfortune as he was tending to his kitchen garden in 1913. On that day, the little fire that he had lit to burn litter was abruptly swept by the blowing wind and eventually burned all the buildings and other properties that Rev. Bans had left behind. He left Zungu (the centre set by Rev. Bans), and walked to Kisauni, Freretown where he sought an audience with the then CMS Secretary, the Rev. Canon H. K. Binns, and sought immediate help in order to reconstruct the destroyed ruins. Without a European resident missionary, it took a long time before a comprehensive response was given. Having seen the brutalities of slavery and the slave trade in the area which had taken place for many years, his uneducated brothers advised him to run and hide, "don't trust these foreigners, they will soon take you into slavery."

Additionally, having heard about the burial of the six "vestal virgins" of neighboring Changamwe, who were buried alive as a warning signal that Christianity was not welcome in the region, the fear Mwagauchi felt escalated. In this context, Mwagauchi's brothers' fears can easily be understood. To ensure that their brother (Mwagauchi) was not buried alive in the public square as in the case of the six virgins, they cautioned him to stop following the European missionaries and hide in a safer area. After both the teacher (Rev. Bans) and his leading student (Mwagauchi) left the region, nothing more has been written about him. In other words, it's not clear where they finally settled. Did Mwagauchi move to another Mijikenda homeland to avoid becoming "enslaved" by the European missionaries? Did Mwagauchi fail to understand the difference between Muslim Arabs and European missionaries? As noted here, did Rev. Bans abandon church ministry and returned to Europe where he settled into a quiet life? Were they traumatized by the Digo mission? Was the Digo mission jinxed? Whatever steps they took, they still remain the heroes of the elusive Digo mission. Certainly, Rev. Bans' efforts were not in vain, despite his most brilliant student undergoing misfortunes that led him to also surrender and disappear from the scene.

Of importance is the fact that the mission which started in 1904, did not die completely with the disappearance of the its key leaders (Bans and his student, Mwagauchi) as Bans' other students, such as Stephen Gude Zani (1899-1985), who later became the leading catechist/evangelist in Digo land, carried out extraordinary duties, such as opening worship centres, even though he had not undergone theological training and was never ordained as a priest. Zani's other classmates in Rev. Bans' class included his brother Mwazani, Lung'anzi, and others who raised the flag of Christ in Digo land till their grandchildren were later able to pick up from where they had left off.

Additionally, four leading families in Digoland stood out and embraced Christianity down to the present. They include: the Ramtu family (providing Ven. Canon Elijah Kubeta Mwahuruma Ramtu, Julia Kusichana, Grace Ramtu, Samuel Hatua Ramtu, Joseph Ramtu, and Timothy Ramtu among others), the Maneno family (providing Samuel Maneno, Rev. Simeon Pore Maneno, and Dr. Maneno among others), the Zani family (producing Elizabeth Zani among others), and the Mwalonya family (producing the likes of Shadrack Mwalonya among others). After undergoing the rigors of Western education, these four families in Digo land turned out to be beacons of light locally and nationally as some served the national government in senior positions, while others served in high ecclesiastical positions. Rev. Bans' work was not in vain. By the time the CMS sent another CMS missionary, Rev. George Wright, to revive the Digo mission in 1914, the flag of Christ was still being lifted by these four families, most of whom were Bans' students.

Ven. Canon Elijah Kubeta Mwahuruma Ramtu

Another critical hero in the Digo mission is Kubeta Mwahuruma Ramtu. Born on June 6, 1936, in Matuga-Mnyenzeni, in the present day Kwale County, Ramtu was the fourth son of Mzee Mwahuruma Ramtu. He joined Waa Primary School in 1952. In an interview, Ramtu recalled that he was one of the eight "lucky" boys who moved to the Standard Three in 1952. Considering that the local culture did not view Western education as an ideal thing to do, he saw himself as being among the lucky ones. In 1954, Kubeta Mwahuruma, as he was then called, sat for his Common Entrance Examination and scored good grades which enabled his admission to the Standard Five at Kwale Intermediate School. At Kwale Intermediate School, he was baptized and renamed Elijah in 1957 (Ramtu 2018). He was baptized by Bishop Ronald Mung'ong'o, the then presiding Bishop of the Methodist Church, though he was an Anglican. By this time, the Mombasa Anglican Diocesan Bishop (Nzano) had allowed Bishop Mung'ong'o to baptize Ramtu on his behalf.

In regard to the system of education (4-4-2-2) that was replaced by 7-4-2-3 (1965) and 8-4-4 in 1985, a person had to undergo 4 years in lower primary school, after which a Common Entrance Exam was taken. Four years in upper primary school (Intermediate) followed, after which the Kenya African Primary Education (KAPE) was completed by African students while Asian students (Indians and Arabs) did a superior education/exam. In turn, the European children did their

Kenya European Primary Education, which was supposed to be the most superior. In other words, Kubeta Mwahuruma studied during the colonial era when the colour-bar (Kenyan apartheid) reared its ugly head, even in educational matters that affected school-aged children (Gathogo 2008).

After the Kenya African Primary Education in Standard Eight, one was expected to go to Junior Secondary School (Form One and Two) and eventually sit for Kenya Junior Secondary Education (KJSE); after which the bright ones proceeded to Form Three and Four for another two years, hence the 4-4-2-2 system (Gathogo 2008). This did not however give room for University education, especially for the African children. Form Four was seen as the highest level of education that one was to undergo. Nonetheless, Elijah Kubeta Ramtu passed well and joined Shimo La Tewa Secondary School in Form One. Upon successful completion of his secondary school education, Ramtu was employed as an Assistant Road Supervisor in Kwale for five years. He later became a Hostel Master for St. Augustine Primary School in Mombasa - a one year position. He then moved back to the Roads Ministry and worked with a private company for three months, and afterwards he started farming (Ramtu 2018). While farming, the call to serve in the Anglican Church as parish priest, became much stronger than before. This eventually led to his joining St. Paul's United Theological College, now St. Paul's University, Limuru, in January 1972. In 1974, he was made an Anglican Deacon; and in the following year, 1975, he was ordained by the then Bishop of Mombasa, Peter Mwang'ombe. He retired in June 2001 at the second highest level after the Diocesan Bishop, the Vicar-General.

Canonically, the Vicar General is the ecclesiastical leader who comes immediately below the Bishop. In the absence of the Diocesan Bishop, the Vicar-General acts on ecclesiastical matters. That is, he or she can organize an invitation to another Bishop to lead in the consecration of a Church building or confirm candidates who are prepared for the rite of confirmation. He can also invite another Bishop, in consultation with the serving Diocesan Bishop, to guide a clergy chapter (Mararo 2018). As the first African clergymen from Digo land, Ven. Canon Elijah Ramtu set a standard for the incoming clergy, and indeed his contribution in the Digo mission remains a challenge for the newest group of ecclesiastical leaders. He does not only climax the ministries of Rev. Bans and Rev.

Binns but he also signals the buoyant future of the Digo mission. His elevation raises several issues: First, will the Digo missionary area be an Anglican Diocese, with a local Diocesan Bishop? Second, will more clergy in the east coast come from the former Diocesan area one day? Such possibilities are potential implications of his ecclesiastical role.

During the 1994 Bishopric elections, where Bishop Julius Kalu was elected, Ramtu was one of the leading candidates. Coming from a mission that appeared jinxed, his 27 years of faithful ministry symbolizes hope for masses of people walking through the valleys of hopelessness and defeatism. His ordination as the first clergymen from Digo land has an impact like that of the biblical Moses (Numbers 20:10) who was expected to hew water out of stone. Together with the second African clergymen in Digo land (Rev. Simeon Pore Maneno), Canon Ramtu and others before them appear like Moses and Aaron who gathered the assembly in front of the rock. Moses then addressed the gathering and said: "Listen, you rebels [doubters], must we bring you water out of this rock?" (Numbers 20:10). That is, despite the Digo mission appearing rocky, there is light at the end of the tunnel. Ramtu's charisma as a church minister was appreciated locally, nationally, and internationally. Hence the reason he stood in various Anglican provincial boards, including the publishing wing of the Anglican Church, Uzima Press. In her book, *Kenya Under My Skin*, Elisabeth Church (1988), who came from England but once visited Kenya, had generous words for Ramtu, when she captured a conversation with her visiting colleagues. She wrote,

> "There is an English Service at Malindi this Sunday. Would you like to come? I hope the Archdeacon is preaching." We accepted gladly. Roddy had told us about the Rev. Elijah Ramtu, Archdeacon of Malindi, whose English was so clear and good that the services could be enjoyed by African and European alike. "Whatsoever he saith unto you do it," was the text of his [Ramtu's] sermon, taken from the story of our Lord turning the water into wine at the marriage feast. "We must do what he tells us, whatever the cost. We must obey the Lord. He is telling us to resist corruption and bribery. If your leg is diseased you can cut it off, if your arm is diseased you can cut it off – but if the disease is in your head …?"

> The Archdeacon [Ramtu] was clearly challenging those in the corridors of power who were corrupt. It was a courageous sermon preached by a man who had clearly counted the cost of obedience himself. Through him we were again reminded of the robust nature of the African church (Church 1988:61).

Rev. Simeon Pore Maneno (1949 -)

The second indigenous person to be ordained as an Anglican priest, after Elijah Kubeta Mwahuruma Ramtu, is Simeon Pore Maneno. Born in 1949, Rev. Maneno studied at Kwale D. E. B. Primary School from 1957 to 1964. He joined Kwale Secondary School in 1966 and completed his O-Levels in 1969. He was absorbed by the Teachers Service Commission (TSC), as an untrained teacher and given his TSC number as 088869, in 1970. He was immediately deployed as a primary school teacher from 1970 to 1989. In 1989, he joined Kagumo Teachers' College, in present-day Nyeri County. At Kagumo College, he graduated with a Diploma in Education (Art and Design, and Christian Religious Education). He could not join Shanzu Teachers' College or Lukore Secondary School as the TSC wanted. Rather, his interest in the Digo mission drove him to insist that he would go to Lungalunga Secondary School (in Digo land) where he taught from 1991 to 1996.

In 1996, he started ailing, probably due to overwork, and subsequently requested a transfer to a centre near his home village. This caused the TSC to deploy him to Perani Primary School. From his village home to Perani School, a distance of 200 metres, it would take about 10 minutes, a big relief for a workaholic. In 2004, Simeon Pore Maneno retired officially with the Teachers' Service Commission, at the age of 55, and joined the Anglican Church on a full time basis. He was posted as a vicar at St. Paul's Church, Ukunda, until 2007 when he retired again, now as a Church minister. Since then, he worked with community services in diverse ways. In one case, he became the Chairman of Peace and Security in Msambweni district (covering Msambweni and Lungalunga which are now two sub-counties). When both were elevated as separate sub-counties, he was left over Lungalunga, as chair. By 2018, he was serving several non-governmental organizations (NGOs). Such NGOs included:

Kwale County Natural Resources Network - as chairman of Lungalunga branch, Muslims for Human Rights (MHURI) – as co-ordinator for Lungalunga sub-county, Kenya Water, Agriculture, and Sanitation Network (KEWASNET) – as co-ordinator of Lungalunga sub-county; URAIA as co-ordinator and civic educator of Lungalunga sub-county, and other social associations within Digo land (Maneno 2018).

While working with the Teachers Service Commission (TSC), an arrangement was made between Bishop Crispus Nzano, Maneno, and his employer that he go for theological training for three years, but resume his teaching duties and serve as school chaplain in the vast Digo missionary area (Kwale county). Therefore he attended St. Paul's United Theological College, Limuru (now St. Paul's University) from 1982 to 1984. He was made an Anglican Deacon in 1984 and ordained by Bishop Nzano in 1985. While still with the TSC, he served at St. Paul's, Makupa and also did Chaplaincy duties at the neighboring Coast Bible School, later renamed Bishop Hannington Institute, College of Theology and Development, which moved from Makupa to Buxton in 1990. Before Coast Bible School was transferred to Makupa in 1956, it was first housed at Mombasa Memorial Cathedral. While at Makupa in 1985, Rev. Maneno also taught Homiletics and Christian Worship. But in 1986, he left Makupa and returned to his teaching career as was initially agreed upon. It is here that he was posted as the Headmaster of Mgombezi Primary School, Lungalunga. He also carried out church duties as a missionary and chaplain to the vast Digo land area.

Regarding his marital status, Rev. Maneno married Elizabeth Jumwa, the daughter of Justus Kalama Lewa and Naomi Dama in 1979. Together, they bore Mercy, Baraka, Johana, and Emmanuel. Elizabeth Jumwa retired as an early childhood development education (ECDE) teacher in 2013 after serving for 42 years. As an ECDE teacher, Elizabeth stands out as an unsung heroine whose role remained unrecognized, but had a huge impact as she sought to mold young children morally and intellectually. Her care for the family and her busy husband in particular led to his huge accomplishments in Digo land. It is no wonder that Rev. Maneno received a presidential award on October 20, 2013 for his contribution to general society, and the Digo people in particular. While the church has never honoured him, nor honoured Elizabeth, the rest of society has met its side of the bargain.

In his proposal and vision for the Digo mission in 1986, which he gave to Bishop Nzano while a missionary *cum* school teacher, he proposed a dramatic growth of the Digo mission by the year 2000. By then, the Digo mission was constituted by only one parish under one clergy member. Rev. Maneno was another clergyman within the Digo mission before 1992. Hence the vast area had only one vicar and a missionary/chaplain *cum* school teacher. Was the mission neglected? As time wore on, Kalume saw the church grow in Digo land, as more parishes were created. For instance, a second parish was created in 1992. It was called Kwale parish and was headed by Rev. Benjamin Buko as its first priest. It was practically all of Kwale County except the Shimba Hills which formed the other parish under Rev. Nyamawi. With Rev. Maneno serving as a missionary in the Kwale Diocesan missionary area, the vast Digo mission now had a total of three clergyman. In 1993, another parish, Kinango, was created under Evangelist Amukhane. In 1994, the Msambweni, Ukunda, and Diani parishes were created within the Digo mission as Rev. Maneno heroically watched with a sense of satisfaction. Further, Mwangwei parish under Rev. Nelson Ndoro and Lungalunga parish under Rev. Ndara were also created. After his retirement from the TSC and upon reaching the then mandatory age of 55 (2004), now 60, he was posted as the vicar of St. Paul's Ukunda till he retired in 2007. Having seen the impracticality of one clergy member serving this vast area, and having voiced his concerns as early as 1986, Pore Maneno's vision was paying dividends. Clearly, as Lupita Ny'ong'o, the Kenyan actress, and the winner of an Oscar award in 2014, noted, "all dreams are valid." There is still room for more dreams for the Digo mission.

Despite the overall statistics of Digo land, which show that Christians are below 2% of the population, it is critically important to appreciate that Anglicans constitute 30%, Independents 35%, Orthodox 0.0%, Other Christians 0.0%, Protestants beside Anglicans 25%, and Roman Catholics 10% (Joshuah 2018). The figures show that Anglicans and Independents are in the majority within Digo land despite the low figures for Christianity in general, as opposed to Islam and traditionalists. The 30% of the Anglicans is due, partly, to the 8 bishops who have served Mombasa since 1884 (Hannington, Parker, Tucker, Peel, Heywood, Crabble, Beecher, Mwang'ombe, Nzano, Kalu, and now Baya). In appointing Rev. Simeon Pore Maneno as the head of the Diocesan Missionary Area in Digo land in 1986, which lasted till 2007 when he retired, Bishop Crispus Nzano, the second African Diocesan Bishop of Mombasa, had a very good strategy for this "difficult" mission. That is, "send a Digo to soften the Anglican mission in Digo land," so as to indigenize and localize the Anglican mission and eventually "soften" it positively, particularly as the church focuses on the Digo mission. Even though Rev. Maneno remained a tentmaker clergyman who was a teacher under the government payroll (Teachers Service Commission, with a TSC No. 088869), he made a huge contribution to the Digo mission as he ministered to the entire Kwale County. As he began to steward the entire Kwale county, which was a mere parish in 1985, he would trek to Lunga Lunga, Matuga, Kinango, Kwale Town, Vyongwane (his home area), among other places though he was stationed at Mgombezi in the Lunga Lunga area. At the time, there were limited vehicles, and indeed, roads were often not passable for cars. Rev. Maneno would serve the Digo who formed the majority in Msambweni, Lunga Lunga, and Matuga subcounties. He was also a missionary to the Duruma ethnic group, who are the dominant group in Kinango sub-county. Additionally, he would serve the migrant Kamba ethnic groups which also have a commanding presence in Kinango and Lunga Lunga just as he ministered to Digo.

As noted earlier, Rev. Simeon Pore Maneno wrote a ground breaking proposal to Bishop Nzano in 1986. In this proposal, which was more of his vision for the Digo mission, he proposed that the entire Digo mission area should have 28 to 30 congregations and have 12 to 18 parishes by the year 2000. Rev. Maneno had also proposed that there be two Archdeaconries and 8 Rural Deaneries by the year 2000. He then requested Bishop Nzano to help him reach his "ambitious" dream, as he sought to dismantle the status quo. Considering that the entirty of Kwale County, as we know it today, was one big parish with one vicar, Rev. Samuel Nyamawi, and Rev. Maneno as the only missionary, the need to expand the ministry further was clearly a good dream. For an area which had only two serving clergymen in 1986, the dream of having over 30 clergy in a span of 14 years was a tall order that Rev. Maneno had. Nevertheless, the entire missionary area had two Archdeaconries (Shimba Hills headed by the Venerable Nelson Mwanjala and Matuga headed by the Venerable Dr. Bryson Samboja) by 2018. It also had two Deaneries: Shimba Hills Deanery headed by Rev. Nelson Ndoro and Likoni Deanery headed by Rev. Peter Mwangi. Further, by 2018, the former Diocesan area had 15 parishes. Matuga Archdeaconry, consisted of the following parishes by 2018: Kwale, Kinango, Ukunda, St. Philipps Likoni, St. John's Mtongwe, St. Paul's Majengo Mapya, St. Stephen Jadini and Waa sub-parish. Shimba Hills Archdeaconry consisted of Shimba Hills, Mwaluvanga, Mafisini, Lukore, Msambweni, Mwangwei, and Lungalunga parishes (Mwangi 2018). In other words, although Rev. Maneno's dream (1986) of 18 parishes and 8 Rural Deaneries has not yet been achieved, the current scenario doesn't paint a faint picture; rather, the buoyancy of a hopeful future remains.

Other heroes and heroines

While it is difficult to capture all of the heroes and heroines in the Digo mission, it is critical to appreciate that there are others, such as Mrs. Robert Matano (a former Cabinet minister's widow), Caroline Tavikala Nimaneno (wife of Stephen Gude Chingiro Zani, the pioneer Catechist), Mariam Kadumbo and her son Albert Matano, Samuel Lugo Dzinendo and his grandson John Lugo, Jonathan Mwapheku (evangelist of the Methodist church), Rev. Nimrod Mboje (buried within the church compound of St. Mathias Anglican Church), and the current ministers (evangelists, catechists, and clergy) of the various churches who are not willing to quit, despite the hardships, financial constraints and domination of other religious groups.

Conclusion

This chapter has retraced the heroes and heroines of the Digo mission by examining it from its founders, the CMS in general, Rev. Bans as the first resident European missionary, Rev. Binns who surveyed the area quietly and supported it in kind as the CMS secretary; successive bishops of Mombasa and the gallant evangelists (starting with Mwagauchi, who was eventually scared off, Stephen Gude Zani who withstood the odds and opened several worship centres, and others). This chapter has also recalled the martyrdom of the six virgins in Bahati-Changamwe, Mombasa in 1912, to frighten and eventually dissuade people in various parts of the East Coast of Africa from accepting any other religion except Islam. As a result of their sacrifice, they ironically brought more to faith in Christianity than was ever envisaged by their killers. This echoes the words of Tertullian who wrote in the year 197 AD/CE, "The blood [of the martyrs] is the seed of Christianity." In chronicling the pioneer African clergy (Ramtu and Maneno), this chapter has sought to celebrate their lives, as no movement is without dedicated leaders. Indeed, being a Christian priest in an area where Christians were less than 1% of the population was a risky gamble. The courage to cross the bridge of Christianity and their resilience amidst huge odds is indeed an extraordinary gesture that cannot go unnoticed. Such heroes and heroines in the Digo mission are a great investment for the future of African Christianity in the 21st century and beyond.

Chapter 9

Womens' Participation in the Digo Mission
By Lawrence Tsawe-Munga Chidongo

Introduction

Dr. Tsawe-Munga wa Chidongo (2012) introduces his book chapter, "Womens' Participation in the Digo Mission," by stressing that the active involvement of African women in religious activities is a long-lived tradition. For women have, since before the introduction of Islam and Christianity, been engaged in healing, prophesying, and guiding society in the ways of God. Though not in the religious context, Niara Sudarkasa (1986) and others, such as Oseni Taiwo Afisi (2010), explain that pre-colonial African women were always officially recognised due to their positions, responsibilities, and the crucial roles they played in society. Isabel Phiri (2000) stressed the independence of African women, noting their control over their own lives and resources. Despite the active participation of African women in religious activities, a stereotyping attitude has characterised African women as being in the category of "legal minors." As expressed by Sudarkasa (1986:1), "For most of their lives, [African women] fell under the first guardianship of their fathers and then of their husbands."

In reference to the Christian mission in Digo land, Chidongo has found out that significantly, Adigo Christian women contributed a lot to the holistic Christian mission, where value was given to schools, health centres, modern methods of farming, and technical skills. All these were reinforced by the Adigo Christian women who ceaselessly encouraged their children to keep on learning and sensitising their fellow Muslim women to the same ideas. The first women converts to Christianity were able to bring up their children with visions of a changing and progressing society. The rest of the Digo community has been influenced by these few families and embraced formal education. Other Digo women converts to Christianity included: Salome Maneno of Vyongwani Church, Ann Ramtu of Bible Translation and Literacy (a Digo project), Elizabeth Maneno Vyongwani, Beatrice Zani Vyongwani, Salome Maneno Vyongwani, Rev. Asha Manjewa (an ACK priest), Naomi Ramtu, Esther Kwekwe, Mrs. Samboja, Esther Mwaka, Rev. Rhoda Luvuno, Pastor Mariam Kadumbo (PEFA), Rev. Grace Ummi, and Pastor Victoria Musyimi.

Reflecting on the history of the introduction of Christianity in Africa, Rodney Stark (1996:133) has similar sentiments as mentioned above, that, "modern and ancient historians agree that women were especially recognized in the early Christian movement." However, there is a need to analyse the styles that missionaries used to reach and win Africans into Christianity, a people who already had their own established beliefs and practices. This study delves into determining the first Digo women that converted to Christianity and their participation in convincing other local women to embrace Christianity.

Christianizing the Coastal Locals

The Digo community belongs to the larger Midzi-Chenda people who comprise the Aduruma, Agiriama, Achonyi, Aravai, Arihe, Akauma, Adzihana, and Akambe. The community shares a common culture and history of immigration. They also share the same myth of creation, that they are all sons and daughters of Muyeye, Mbodze, and Matsezi. The myth of creation, which states that God *Mulungu* first created man and called him Muyeye, then created for him two wives, Mbodze and Matsezi is a source of their identity and unity. Another important story is the myth of their migration from the same land, Shungwaya.

The Adigo live on the south coast of Kenya, along the coastal line in the former Kwale District and present Kwale County; but some are also found in Tanzania: Horohoro and Tanga. Kaingu Kalume

Tinga (2004) and Tsawe-Munga Chidongo (2012, 2018) show that the Midzi-Chenda, the Adigo included, are unquestionably religious, having had the concept of God *Mwenyezi Mungu/Mulungu* before the introduction of Islam and Christianity. Oral Digo history reveals that there lived special religious women prophetesses such as *Nimuyumba* and *Nimahongo* in Digo land who foresaw the coming of foreigners that would introduce new forms of religious beliefs, languages, and cultures. Over time, the prophesies were fulfilled when foreigners who had come for trade also started sharing their religious beliefs, cultures, and systems of governance to the local communities. Martin (1974), Watt (1944) and Pauwels (1978) explain that between 900 to 1300 AD/CE, Islam along the East African coast was introduced to indigenous Africans by trading Arab and Persian migrants (Shirazi from Persia and Arabs from Arabia). "The carriers of the new religion were identified as 'Arabs' descendants of those from Southeast Arabia and the Persian Gulf" (Conn 1978: 75). It can be argued that Islam was established along the coast of Kenya earlier than Christianity. The communities that easily converted to Islam are the Adigo and Aduruma from the south coast.

On the other hand, John Baur (1994) argues that Christianity in coastal Kenya might have been introduced as early as the fourth century by monks thought to have come from Ethiopia. Baur (1994) explains that the early efforts of the Ethiopian monks never flourished due to several campaigns of resistance created by the hostile Ethiopian Galla "Oromo" people. For the purpose of this chapter, the Digo first women Christian converts, we cannot rely on the argument by Baur because there are no traces of Christianity that were left by the Ethiopian monks. There is a higher probability that the Roman Catholic Portuguese who came in the 16th century under the influence of Vasco Da Gama could have introduced Christianity to the southern coast of Kenya. According to Thomas Spear (1978), this was the same period when the Nyika community was in transit from Shungwaya. In an interview with Prof. Mwakimako, I gathered that the Adigo community could have embraced Islam in Ethiopia during their transit from Congo. When they arrived on the coast in the 16th Century, they became hesitant in accepting Christianity due to its many doctrinal restrictions. However, Mwakimako mentioned that the argument of the Adigo having been Islamised in Ethiopia is debatable. In fact there is no mention of Islam from Ethiopia in Thomas Spears' (1978) research or by others such as

Cynthia Brantley, David Parkin, Zeleza Tiyambe, and Patterson. Despite these noted gaps, it cannot be doubted that the 16th century phase of Christian missionaries on the coast of Kenya and in East Africa in general, faced resistance due to the already existing and deep rooted beliefs of Islam. According to Baur (1994) and Zablon Nthamburi (1982), in the 200 years of Portuguese dominance on the coast of Kenya, Africans experienced religious hostility, slavery, and being forced to become Christians, including the Arabs of Mombasa and Malindi. Baur explains,

> In 1500, two years after da Gama, a second navigator named Cabral called in at Kilwa [and Mombasa] on his way to India. On board, he had eight Franciscans, eight chaplains and one vicar (a parish priest). He had been given the royal instructions that these priests should first use their spiritual sword before he thought of using the secular one. But if the Moors [Muslims] and pagans did not accept the Christian faith and refused the offered peace and commerce, he should wage war against them with fire and sword. (Baur 1994: 87)

The indications are clear that the Portuguese period in coastal Kenya was not a peaceful one as there were frequent intense struggles with the Arabs over the acquiring of trade stations, as well as over forced conversions to Christianity. History shows that on August 21, 1631, Yusufu al Hassan (Jeromino), whose father had been killed by the Portuguese in a spirit of revenge, staged a campaign that meant to stamp out Christianity in Mombasa by killing 288 Christians. Seventy-two of the slain were African men with their wives and children. It is not known whether any Digos were present among the Seventy-two killed, but it is logical to assume there were because some Nyika families were close to the Island of Mombasa, living in Chaani, Miritini, Magongo, and Changamwe (Chimera 2018) then. The scenario was a traumatic one for close relatives of those slain who might have survived the massacre.

By early 1700, the Portuguese were overpowered by Arabs from Oman. This time round, Muslim Arabs were determined to turn the coastal region back to Islam, but there were impediments as a Protestant Christian revival movement in Europe in the 19th Century was scheming on how to win souls for Christ in the same region. Within this same period, a cry from Christians such as William Wilberforce had risen to campaign to end the slave trade. The steps that were taken to abolish the slave trade became factors that triggered new missionary activities on the coast of East Africa and in Kenya in particular. This drives us to find out more about how women participated in the Digo Christian Mission. There were various Protestant Christian Associations such as; the Church Missionary Society (CMS), the United Free Methodist Mission (UMM), the Church of Scotland Mission (CSM), the London Mission Society (LMS), the Holy Ghost Fathers (HGF), and the African Inland Mission (AIM) that brought missionaries in order to convert locals to Christianity. The leading missionary was the renowned Dr. David Livingstone. Others that followed were Dr. Johann Ludwig Krapf, Johannes Rebman, Thomas Wakefield, and Charles New.

During the missionary work of the 19th Century, it is highly likely that the Midzi-Chenda were scared of the religious differences due to the previous unpleasant experiences, such as the killings of Christians at Fort Jesus. In our discussion with some Adigo elders at Kwale Golden Guest House on October 10, 2018, concerning the reasons for the slow pace of Christianity in Digo land, there were repeated statements from the elders (Canon Ramtu and Mzee Maneno) who expressed the view that there was a past event where a virgin girl from Digo land and another group of 6 virgins were buried alive so as to invoke the spirits, so that the (Adigo) should never embrace Christianity. The elders were very categorical that this happened, but could not tell us where it happened. Among the elders, some said that this event happened in Changamwe, but others insisted that it was in Digo land. Canon Ramtu explained that some family members of a man who saw the event as it happened were still alive; one being the first wife of the former member of parliament of the Kinango constituency (the late Stanley Robert Matano). According to the elders, it is believed that this kind of religious ritual is irreversible (*muiko*). I had some interest in interviewing a renowned Islamic historian, Prof. Hassan Mwakimako, who held the view that it was hard to reach a conclusion if such an event took place, as there are various complications (Mwakimako 2018). It actually depends on who the giver of the information was and also the context. As mentioned earlier, Mwakimako (2018) also pointed out the fact that Islam on the coast came very early, and was embraced by the south coast community because of the diverse factors that seemed to favour the culture of the community. Christianity among the Adigo was accepted on some grounds of Western education, which the majority of the Adigo rejected. The few families that embraced Christianity were looked down upon by the rest and were considered as outcasts. The story of the virgins being buried alive could be allegations to justify the small numbers of Christian converts among the Adigo, or it may be a true story that drives us to do further research on this topic. Like with the rest of the Midzi-Chenda, the Adigo did not practice human sacrifice.

I had time to interview Prof. Rocha Chimera of Pwani University with regard to the issue of Muslims burying virgin girls alive. Chimera was of the view that the Adigo during the 16th century had settled at Mtongwe, Ngombeni, and some parts of Kwale. They had left the Aduruma at Mazeras (Ganjoni) taking care of animals in the surroundings of Kaya Mtswakara. But the probability that it took place also depends on the one who told the story. He did confirm the killings of Christians by Yusufu al Hassan (Jeromino) in August 1631. Mr. Ali Wasi Mwabaya had a different view, that there are some Kiswahili accounts, which I could not easily access, that have hinted about the killing of six Changamwe virgins.

Biblical Influence on Women's Participation

Women in the New Testament played critical roles in the support of Jesus' mission and propagation of the Christian faith. Christoph Stenschke (2009) explains that a number of women are recipients of the benefactions of Jesus and his disciples. Jesus' style of mission seemed to rely on women and their families more than men. While the scriptures are silent on whether the women who were close to Jesus' mission (such as Mary Magdalene, Salome Zebedee, and others) were single, married or divorced, the significant point is that they offered their active participation. In the early Church's mission (cf. Philipians 4:2), there is a mention of Eudia and Syntyche who struggled beside Paul in the work of the gospel together with a number of men. In Acts 1:14, 9:31, Luke mentions other women such as Tabitha and Saphira who were active in mission work. They were active in Jerusalem and Damascus, and also assisted in planting the churches throughout Judea, Galilee and Samaria, in Lydda, and in Joppa, as far as Antioch. Paul also involved women in planting churches (cf. Colossians 4:17). Women's (family) houses were frequently used by Jesus and by Paul for mission work. Lydia of Philippi an "Eastern business woman turned to be a Christian heroine" when she hosted Christian missionaries. Believers met at the house of Mary, the mother of John Mark, where her house was used for evangelistic purposes. No wonder that from Biblical studies and church history, Henry Chadwick (1967:56) noted that, "Christianity seems to have been especially successful among women. It was often through the wives that it penetrated the upper classes of society in the first instance."

Some pioneering Christian missionaries of the 19th century in coastal Kenya came with their wives, while others came single. The techniques that were used by Jesus, Paul, and early church missionaries, of approaching families first, may have been applied to evangelize the Adigo community. It has to be noted that the Adigo are a matriarchal community, therefore, womens' (*fuko*) voice and decisions were more weightily considered than those of men (*mbari*). In our discussion with the elders from the Digo community, we were able to identify five families that converted to Christianity in the early 1900s. These families were: Ramtu, Zani, Maneno, Mwalonya and Lugo. It will be of significance to have an understanding of what drove them to convert to Christianity.

Digo Women and Their Participation

The first missionaries who are remembered to have come to the south coast were Rev. Bans and Binns. The Ramtu family had settled at Matuga Nganasani. The missionaries made a camp and stayed with the family members for some time. Two young brothers who had trained as carpenters at Waa Polytechnic, Mwarasiwa Ramtu and Mwahuruma Ramtu, were converted, given Christian teachings, were baptised, and given new names "Joseph" for Mwarasiwa and "Stephen" for Mwahuruma. They had a young sister called N'rasiwa who also converted, was baptised and given a new name "Grace." She now became Grace N'rasiwa. In turn, Grace N'rasiwa is not well remembered, because according to an explanation by Cannon Elija Ramtu, she died before being married. When Mwarasiwa reached the age of marriage, he was advised to find a Christian girl within the community. Subsequently, he fell in love with Elizabeth Nizani. They then were married and eventually gave birth to two daughters; Grace Nilihunga who was married at Vyongwani and

Naomi In'chamwitu who was married at Kinango. In an interview, family members explained that Mrs. Elizabeth Mwarasiwa Ramtu was a woman who took her Christian values seriously, and was keen to inculcate her children with Christian morals as they grew up. She was an advisor but also lived as a model of reflection for the Digo community. Another woman from the Ramtu family, who came after Elizabeth, is Naomi Ramtu.

Joseph Mwahuruma Ramtu may not have been a dynamic Christian, but he went on with the Christian faith. He married a non-Christian girl, Mwanamisi Chitsango, who later converted to Christianity and became a model for her children. Reverend Cannon Elijah Ramtu is a son of Joseph Mwahuruma and Ann Mwanamisi Ramtu. For the two families, their daughters became pioneers in acquiring education. Rachael Bahati Ramtu and Christine In'dzanache Ramtu became qualified teachers with a PI grade. Their charisma both for education and Christianity was gradually felt by other Digo women who finally decided to allow their children to go to school.

The Maneno family started with Juma, who was recruited by the Kenya Africa Rifles (KAR) and was trained for war. He later underwent catechist training and was baptized, and subsequently renamed "John." John Juma Maneno had a sister called Caroline Tavikala Nimaneno, who also embraced Christianity. John Juma married In'kutawala, who converted to Christianity when she had a family. She was baptised and given a new name, "Mary." Mary Maneno, as in the case of Elizabeth, was keen to bring up her family in the Christian doctrines. Gradually, the family provided key people in education and the civil service who also served the entire nation of Kenya. However, Mary Maneno is less mentioned in the activities of the Church despite her efforts to live by example.

The other family is that of Zani which had settled at Vyongwani. All of the elders insisted that this was the place where the first church among the Adigo was planted. The patriarch of the family, Mr. Randani Mwadebwe Zani, did not embrace Christianity, but was kind enough to allow his children to join the new religion; an act that was not common among Muslim Digos. From the family, there was a young man called Chingoro Gude Zani. He was also converted and baptised after undergoing catechism classes. He was named "Stephen." Cannon Elijah Ramtu conceded that Stephen Gude was the first Mdigo catechist/evangelist. Gude also underwent an ordained-ministerial-training at a Christian theological ministerial school in Kisauni-Freretown, but could not be admitted into the ordained ministry. Gude was married to Caroline Tavikala Nimaneno. Caroline Tavikala, having come from an established Christian family, was more enlightened about the benefits of Christianity. She became a model in Digo land after she established a Christian family that was admired by many people. Her daughters, for example Nelly Zani, Sophie, Lizzy, and Margaret were symbols of unity, and they were married within the vast Midzi-Chenda community.

Concluding sentiments

Significantly, Adigo Christian women contributed a lot to holistic Christian mission. Value was given to schools, health centres, modern methods of farming, and technical skills. All these were reinforced by the Adigo Christian women who ceaselessly encouraged their children to keep on learning and sensitising their fellow Muslim women to do the same. The first women converts to Christianity were able to bring up their children with visions of a changing and progressing society. The rest of the Digo community has been influenced by these few families and embraced formal education. Other contributions to Christianity from the Digo women converts included those from: Salome Maneno of Vyongwani Church, Ann Ramtu of Bible Translation and Literacy (a Digo project), Elizabeth Maneno Vyongwani, Beatrice Zani Vyongwani, Salome Maneno Vyongwani, Rev. Asha Manjewa (an ACK priest), Naomi Ramtu, Esther Kwekwe, Mrs. Samboja, Esther Mwaka, Rev. Rhoda Luvuno, Pastor Mariam Kadumbo (PEFA), Rev. Grace Ummi, and Pastor Victoria Musyimi. Women in the Mwalonya family and Lugo have not appeared in this list, which points to the gaping holes in the research about the Digo mission. In turn, this drives us to do further research on Adigo Christian converts, and especially the contribution of women in the last 114 years (1904-2018).

Chapter 10

Protestants and Pentecostal Churches: A Survey

By Joshua Itumo Kiilu

Introduction

Apart from the Anglican and the Methodist Churches, there are other Protestant churches that have been operating in Digo land since 1904, though some came recently. There are others whose ecclesiastical model is Pentecostal, Charismatic, or African Instituted Churches. Generally, Pentecostalism and its offshoots can be divided into three groups: "Classical" Pentecostals, those who are members of the standard Pentecostal groups, most of which originated in the first quarter of the twentieth century; the Charismatics, or those in other denominations who received the "baptism of the Holy Spirit;" and the so-called "Neo-Charismatics," the groups formed in the last half of the 20th century, most of which are not affiliated with the Pentecostal denominations.

In Kenya, the Pentecostal movement emerged in the 1960s, and differs significantly from the five ecclesiastical structures that emerged after the 16th century Reformation in Europe (Mugambi 1995). Among these structures are: the Episcopal model where power and authority are vested in the bishop; the Presbyterian model which is based on references in the New Testament to the elders who provided guidance and leadership in the apostolic Christian communities; the Congregational model where power and authority are vested in the entire congregation; the Pentecostal model where emphasis is on possession by the Holy Spirit, particularly as evidenced by speaking in tongues, rather than to individuals and councils; and the Charismatic model where the emphasis is on charismatic gifts (1 Cor. 12:1ff) such as wisdom, knowledge, faith, healing, working of miracles, prophecy, discerning of spirits, speaking in tongues, interpretation of tongues, and so forth. Of course there is a very thin line between the latter two.

General Characteristics

In many parts of the world, Pentecostals are notorious for rather aggressive forms of evangelism and proselytism, and Africa is no exception. Though the word proselytism originally referred to Early Christianity (and earlier Gentiles such as God-fearers), it now refers to the attempt of any religion or religious individuals to convert people to their beliefs, or any attempt to convert people to a different point of view, religious or not. From its beginning, the Pentecostal movement was characterised by an emphasis on evangelistic outreach, and Pentecostal mission strategy placed evangelism as its highest priority. Evangelism meant to go out and reach the "lost" for Christ in the power of the Holy Spirit. The beginnings of North American Pentecostalism in the Azusa Street revival of Los Angeles resulted in a category of ordinary but "called" people called "missionaries" fanning out to every corner of the globe within a remarkably short space of time. "Mission" was mainly understood as "foreign mission" (mostly from "white" to "other" peoples), and these missionaries were mostly untrained and inexperienced. Their only qualification was the baptism in the Spirit and a divine calling. Their motivation and task was to evangelise the world before the imminent coming of Christ, and so evangelism was more important than education or "civilisation" (Hollenweger 1972:34). Pentecostal missiologist Grant McClung says that early Pentecostals had a "last day's mission theology" as follows: "Premillennialism, dispensationalism, and the belief in the imminency of Christ's return forged the evangelistic fervor of the movement in its infancy" (McClung 1986:51). Premillennialism rose to prominence in the late 19th century, and the idea that the gospel must be preached to all nations before the imminent return of Christ was fuelled by the *Scofield Reference Bible* and the writings of A. B. Simpson, both popular among Western Pentecostals at least until the 1970s (Dempster, Klaus & Petersen 1991:207).

Gary McGee (1994) describes the first 20 years of Pentecostalism as mostly "chaotic in operation." Reports filtering back to the West to garnish newsletters would be full of optimistic and triumphalistic accounts of how many people were converted, healed, and had received Spirit baptism, seldom mentioning any difficulties encountered or the inevitable cultural blunders made. Early Pentecostal missionaries from North America and Europe were mostly paternalistic, often creating dependency, and sometimes they were even racist (McGee 1994: 208, 211). There were notable exceptions to this general chaos, however. As Willem Saayman (1993: 42, 51) has observed, most Pentecostal movements "came into being as missionary institutions" and their mission work was "not the result of some clearly thought out theological decision, and so policy and methods were formed mostly in the crucible of missionary praxis." It must be acknowledged that despite the seeming naiveté of many early Pentecostals, their evangelistic methods were flexible, pragmatic, and astonishingly successful. They claimed that the rapid growth of the Pentecostal movement vindicated the apostle Paul's statement that God uses the weak and despised to confound the mighty. Pentecostal churches all over the world were missionary by nature, and the dichotomy between "church" and "mission" that for so long plagued other Christian churches did not exist. This "central missiological thrust" was clearly a "strong point in Pentecostalism" and central to its existence (Saayman 1993: 42, 51).

This rapid spread was not without its serious difficulties, however. The parochialism and rivalry of many Pentecostal missions made ecumenical co-operation difficult. The tendencies towards paternalism created a reluctance to listen to voices from the Third World, and the need for a greater involvement in the plight of the poor and in opposing socio-political oppression are some of the issues that must be addressed. But in spite of these problems, Pentecostalism today has many lessons for the universal church in its mission.

> The history of Pentecostal missions demonstrates that the Pentecostals have rarely retreated from challenges, affirming dependence on the Holy Spirit to

guide their responses. Their irrepressible advance from obscurity to center stage within ninety years suggests that only the unwary will underestimate their fortitude. (Dempster, Klaus & Petersen 1991: 207)

Pentecostals believe that the coming of the Spirit brings the ability to perform "signs and wonders" in the name of Jesus Christ to accompany and authenticate their evangelism. Pentecostals all over the world, but especially in the Third World, see the role of healing as good news for the poor and afflicted. Early 20th century Pentecostal newsletters and periodicals abounded with "thousands of testimonies to physical healings, exorcisms and deliverances" (Dempster, Klaus & Petersen 1991: 207). McClung says that divine healing is an "evangelistic door-opener" for Pentecostals, and that "signs and wonders" are the "evangelistic means whereby the message of the kingdom is actualized in 'person-centered' deliverance" (McClung 1986: 51). The "signs and wonders" promoted by independent Pentecostal evangelists led to the rapid growth of Pentecostal churches in many parts of the world, although they have seldom been without controversy (Dempster, Klaus & Petersen 1991: 207). The Pentecostal understanding of the preaching of the Word in evangelism was that "signs and wonders" should accompany it, and divine healing in particular was an indispensable part of Pentecostal evangelistic methodology (Dempster, Klaus & Petersen 1991).

Indeed, in many cultures of the world, and especially in Africa, a major attraction for Pentecostalism has been its emphasis on healing. In these cultures, the religious specialist or "person of God" has power to heal the sick and ward off evil spirits and sorcery. This holistic function, which does not separate the "physical" from the "spiritual," is restored in Pentecostalism, and indigenous peoples see it as a "powerful" religion to meet human needs. For some Pentecostals, faith in God's power to heal directly through prayer resulted in a rejection of other methods of healing. The numerous healings reported by Pentecostal evangelists confirmed that God's Word was true, God's power was evident in their efforts, and the result was that many were persuaded to become Christians. This emphasis on healing is so much part of Pentecostal evangelism, especially in Africa, that large public campaigns and tent crusades preceded by great publicity are frequently used in order to reach as many "unevangelised" people as possible. Hollenweger says that Pentecostals are "efficient evangelists" because of "the power of their experience" (Hollenweger 1997: 23). Although we may regard some manifestations of Pentecostalism with amusement, disdain, or even alarm, we dare not ignore this enormous factor in World Christianity.

Pentecostalism in Kenya

Two years before independence, 1960, the renowned international American evangelist, Billy Graham, visited Kenya and in effect began Evangelicalism in Kenya. He was closely followed by another renowned evangelist, T. L. Osborn whose series of crusades gave impetus for open air preaching (Shorter and Njiru 2001: 18, 28). David Barrett has noted that an earlier crusade by Osborn in 1957 at Mombasa led to a "widespread Pentecostal movement" (Barrett 1982: 26). A visit, in 1968, by another Pentecostal preacher, Oral Roberts, and his subsequent healing rallies in Nairobi marked a major turning point in the history and establishment of Pentecostal churches.

Pentecostalism in Kenya and East Africa thus benefited from the existing East African Revival movement, even though the "spirit of Pentecostalism" had been in East Africa from as early as 1895 when the African Inland Mission was first founded in Kenya. Other theories have it that the presence of the Pentecostal Assemblies of God (PAG) can be traced in Kenya from as early as 1938. To this end, crusades by Osborn and others could have catalysed its growth and not necessarily its birth (Shorter and Njiru 2001: 27f). This trend has continued to the present where Pentecostalism has grown by leaps and bounds. It became Afro-Pentecostalism in the 1990s after economic depression hit the people of Kenya. In the ensuing scenario, Pentecostal leadership openly addressed thematic issues such as: poverty is not in the plan of God, sickness does not come from God, God desires a healing society, exorcisms, prosperity, hope amidst despair, and other general social issues were also addressed. Again, healing crusades and the gospel of hope became a common occurrence in both the open air spaces and in the media (Gathogo 2011a: 133-151). After President Daniel Arap Moi's era (1979-2002) came to an end, the leadership of the emerging Christian groups went a step further when they began to participate explicitly in political affairs. In the Constituency Development Fund (CDF) kitties that were began by the Mwai Kibaki (2003-2012) regime, in each of the then 210 constituencies one could hardly see a constituency, particularly in Central Kenya, where one of their leaders was not nominated as a member of the committee that ran the funds. As Kenya embarks on a new system of governance, where the 47 governors steward their respective 47 county governments, the influence of the emerging Christian groups will remain a force to be reckoned with.

Pentecostalism in Digo Land

As in the case of the mainline churches, the first strand of Pentecostalism in Digo land came from Mombasa, the neighboring county. As noted earlier, the renowned international American evangelist, Billy Graham, visited Kenya and in effect brought Evangelicalism to the East African coast, in 1958, and Digo land must have tasted it, though to a very minimal level. As David Barrett has noted, T. L. Osborn's activities on the east coast of Africa, where he preached and held healing sessions in 1957 at Mombasa which led to a "widespread Pentecostal movement" (Barrett 1982: 26). Digo land, like any other part of the coastal region couldn't have escaped the dramatic happenings such as excorcisms, healings, bold preaching, and other events that go with Pentecostalism.

It is from there that the Pentecostal Evangelistic Fellowship (PEFA) began to be held in Mombasa and Digo land, through Elim Evangelistic Church, whose headquarters is at Makupa, Mombasa. Other Elim Evangelistic Churches include: Elim Church (PEFA) Kongowea, Elim Evangelistic Church Pendeza PEFA, Maweu PEFA Church, and PEFA Dabaso Church among others (Maneno 2018, Ramtu 2018). As Samuel Kang'ethe Mwatha (2018) has noted, the Pentecostal Evangelistic Fellowship of Africa (PEFA) was born out of a merger between two missionary agencies, namely: Elim Missionary Assemblies (EMA) and the International Pentecostal Assemblies Missions (IPAM). He goes on to say:

> Both of these bodies were steeped in the theology and practices of classical or traditional Pentecostalism. These two were linked to parent churches in the U.S.A. Elim Missionary Assemblies is now Elim Fellowship and has their headquarters in Lima, New York. As for the International Pentecostal Assemblies, it is now known as

the International Pentecostal Churches of Christ, with its headquarters located in London, Ohio. The combination body, PEFA came into being in 1962 when it was registered with the Kenya Government, after the parent missions released their respective churches into the merger. In Kenya, there were two pioneer locations for PEFA, each representing one of the founding traditions. One was the Elim Bukuria Mission representing the work in Bukuria and Suna-Migori in southwestern Kenya, and the other was the IPA Kaimosi Mission representing work in western Kenya. These two churches merged to form PEFA. (Mwatha 2018)

Other Pentecostal churches that began to appear in the coastal region include: Kenya Assemblies of God (KAG), which split from Elim Evangelistic Church in 1974; and the East African Pentecostal Church. In other words, the first Bishop of the Kenya Assemblies of God, on the East African coast, first served at Elim Evangelistic Church – which is one of the PEFA Churches, before they split. After KAG crossed over to Digo land and spread its branches to Likoni (Harambee area) under the leadership of Joshuah Songa for 7 years, they spread further to Digo land and sent Pastor Simeon Mbuzi, a Digo by ethnic extraction, to steward Migumoni in 1978. Simeon Mbuzi is the father of Bishop Mwarandu of Redeemed Gospel Church (RGC). In turn, Mwarandu took the Redeemed Gospel Church to Shimba Hills, and by 2018, he was still a very powerful televangelist. Mwarandu has also teemed up with the KAG to open more revival centres in Digo land and the rest of the East African coast. In view of this move, the most dominant Pentecostal churches in Digo land are the Kenya Assemblies of God and the Redeemed Gospel Church (RGC).

Another interesting dimension is that the East African Pentecostal Church (EAPC) split from the Pentecostal Evangelistic Fellowship of Africa (PEFA) (Maneno 2018, Ramtu 2018). In comparison, the East African Pentecostal Church is stronger than the PEFA in Digo land. In light of this, there are several observations to make about Digo Pentecostalism. First, Digo Pentecostalism is characterized by splits. Their main challenge is multiple splits, even though they still remain Pentecostal. Second, Digo Pentecostalism is a threat to the mainline churches. Are they fishing from the same basket as their counterparts, the mainline churches? Are they genuinely growing? This Pentecostal growth is more visible in Duruma land than Digo land itself. As a matter of fact, Duruma areas such as Kinango, Mariakani, Samburu, Taru, and Mwena are some of the places where this growth is evident. In Digo land, there is also a minimal sign of Pentecostal growth in areas such as Likoni, Matuga, Msambweni, Shimba Hills, Ukunda, Kwale, and Lungalunga (Maneno 2018, Ramtu 2018).

A case in point is Ushindi Baptist at Likoni, which was started by Pastor Maisha. It came from Moshi, Tanzania. The phenomenal growth of this Pentecostal church, its healing prowess and other activities has sent local people talking, and viewing it from a mixed approach. Nevertheless, the growth of Pentecostalism in Digo land as in the case of the mainline churches is an unstoppable force in the 21st century.

Other Churches in Digo Land

Though not a Pentecostal church, the African Inland Church (AIC) that came as African Inland Mission in 1895, and the only missionary society beholden to American Evangelicalism reached Digo land through immigrants to the area in 1970. This is when Samuel Nganda lived at Makobe as a peasant-farmer and not initially as a pastor. Considering that he was a member of the AIC, he planned to begin the AIC Church with his wife, who had only one child then. They then built a local church at Makobe between 1972 and 1974. They later built another church at a place called Maumba within the Shimba Hills location. Eventually, Samuel Nganda ended up an AIC pastor at Makobe. Even though he did not target the Digos, he was successfully able to reach his fellow Kamba immigrants in Digo land. Finally he reached the Duruma people after interacting with them. This was followed by intermarriages between the Kamba and the Duruma which eventually became a common trend. This eventually led to the establishment of AIC Duruma churches, and AIC Duruma pastors, which continues till today.

In 1945 the independent, African Brotherhood Church (ABC) came in from a place called Mitaboni in Machakoes County. The founder of the ABC was D. Kamollo, a bishop of the African Brotherhood Church. In 1971, the ABC reached the Shimba Hills through a man called M.

Mawess who started the ABC church at Makobe. In 1971-72, the same year he began another church at a place called Mivumoni where he had a *shamba*. In 1976, they began a church at a place called Maumba. The two churches were largely composed of Kamba people. When the Pentecostals "scared" them off, in the 1980s, they changed tactics and went for a mission outreach beyond their ethnic group. Under Bishop Songa of the Kenya Assemblies of God (KAG), which reached Kwale in 1982, two youths were converted from Digo land, namely: Mohammed Jeruman and Bakari Ndoro Mbakari. Mohamed Jerumani, a Digo, went on to become a pastor of the KAG.

Conclusion

This paper has attempted to show the impact of the dramatic entry of Pentecostalism in Digo land that threatens the mainline churches such as the Catholics, Anglicans, and the Methodists, among others. It also shows that the Digo mission has moved beyond Anglicanism as there are now other churches such as the African Brotherhood Church, the Salvation Army, which has been there since the 1970s and was the most powerful and visible church; and also the African Independent or African Instituted Churches, brought by immigrants to Digo land. Such an influx has included pockets of Akorino adherents despite them being a tiny group. In theorizing about Pentecostalism, as a church model, this chapter has attempted to show its indispensability in modern missions to Africa and beyond.

Chapter 11

Challenges and Prospects in Digo Mission
By Julius Gathogo

Introduction

After a long history of Protestant missions began in the East African Coast in 1844 with the arrival of the German Lutheran cleric, Johann Ludwig Krapf (1810-1881), who was serving under the auspices of the Church Missionary Society (CMS), the pioneer European missionary, Rev. Bans, began the Digo Mission in 1904, when he settled as a resident clergyman. Owing to the heavy Islamic and African religious presence in Digo land, it was not possible to start the Digo Mission as in other parts of East Africa. While the CMS missionaries were keen to conquer all regions of the East Coast of Africa for the gospel of Christ, it was not easy for the missionaries to conquer Digo land in present day Kwale County, where the Digo sub-group of the larger Mijikenda community live with their cousin sub-group, the Waduruma.

In total, Mijikenda (also called Midzikenda, meaning nine towns or cities), has nine related clusters of Bantu ethnic sub-groups. This includes the northern Mijikenda: Chonyi, Kambe, Duruma, Kauma, Ribe, Rabai, Jibana, and Giriama; and the Southern Mijikenda: the Digo, who are also found in Tanzania due to their proximity to the common border. In a nutshell, the Mijikenda inhabit the East African coast of Kenya, between the Sabaki and the Umba rivers. The area stretches from the border with Tanzania on the south to the border near Somalia in the north (Baur 1994).

In his first visit to Digo land in 1878 and 1879, Rev. H. K. Binns visited the Malaba area of Kwale County. He was mesmerized by the serenity of the area due to the nearby Godoni forest, though the heavy Islamic presence must have discouraged him from settling there. As a long serving coastal Archdeacon, he was not able to change Digo land and turn them to Christ despite the huge resources that he controlled as the coastal regional CMS secretary from 1899 to 1922. He however played a key *diakonia* (service) role to all, Muslims and traditionalists alike, when he fed over 1000 people with relief food during the 1899 famine that hit the region (Binns 2018).

Another critical point to note is that the population of the Digo people, who are found in both Kenya and Tanzania, stands at 546,478 with the Digo of Kenya constituting 71% (388,000) and Tanzania 29% (158,478). Their most dominant religion in the 21st century is Islam at 79%. Others are traditionalists at 20% while Christian denominations share about 1% of the population (Joshuah 2018). While this chapter will attempt to account for these religious disparities, it is worthwhile to state from the outset that there is a need for any missiologist to target the traditionalist worldview, which constitutes the 20% before employing any other strategy.

Like other mission areas and regions of Kenya, Digo land in Kwale County and beyond experienced a hotchpotch of challenges in its initial stages. It continues to experience new forms of challenges in the 21st century. This chapter addresses such setbacks in the mission of Christ in Digo land. According to the recent Kenyan Situation Population Analysis (SPA 2013), Digo land of Kwale county in Kenya, which also encompasses Duruma land, experiences common challenges such as poverty, fertility and family planning, health systems and service delivery for sexual reproductive health, infant-child and maternal mortality, HIV, sexually transmitted infections, malaria and tuberculosis, youth-status and prospects, marital concerns, emergency situations and humanitarian response, migration and settlement concerns, and the concern for sustainable development among many other issues.

Some Setbacks, Past and Present

A leading evangelist/catechist clergyman from Digo land, Stephen Gude Zani (1899-1985), recalls, in his writing, how the Digo mission began. Zani (1983:1) says:

> In 1904, a European missionary from the UK, by the name of Bans, visited Digo land. He was accompanied by three African assistants; namely Macheche Baraka from Rabai, Njuguna, and Munuhe Munene. The latter two were from Kikuyu land in central Kenya. Bans went on to construct the Pastor's house, then a makeshift house for worship and prayer [temporary church] dug a borehole for fresh water on Mwangala side, and built a teachers' house. He then brought an elderly person by the name Ephraim Yamungu who took care of cattle near the nearby forest. It is from there that Bans started teaching the Digo people. He stayed in this centre for eight years. The centre was renamed Pa Mzungu or Zungu [the European's place].

Stephen Gude (1983) goes on to explain more about the setbacks that hit the Digo mission eight years later. He noted that as Bans taught the Digos only one student (by the name of Mwagauchi) outstandingly understood his lessons, and he eventually became Bans' point man throughout Digo land. Others who became Bans' companions in Digo land include: Zani himself, his brother Mwazani, and Lung'anzi among a few others. Despite all these efforts, Zani was surprised in 1912 when Rev. Bans came to bid farewell to his father as he conceded that the Digo mission was too difficult for him. After that, Zani admitted, they didn't find another teacher. Mwagauchi remained in Zungu as he took care of the coconut, palm, and mango trees. He also took care of the buildings that were left by Bans. Another setback crept in, in 1913, when Mwagauchi lit a fire as he tended his little farm. Unfortunately, it accidentally burnt down everything that Bans had left behind, including parts of the local forest. His abrupt visit to the CMS Kisauni mission centre, where he sought assistance from the regional Secretary, the Rev. Canon H. K. Binns, did not bear fruit as the CMS team took too long to respond to his calls for help. As time wore on, Mwagauchi was dissuaded by his Digo brothers to abandon the European missionaries as they would do harm to him. He was advised to move elsewhere and hide in unknown places as the Europeans were likely to come and capture him and sell him as a slave. Having heard or experienced the slave trade that was championed by both Arabs and the Portuguese previously, Mwagauchi's brothers and the general society could not trust Bans' and Binns' team. This compares to a local saying in colonial central Kenya where the locals' mistrust of the Europeans made them say, "*Gutire muthungu na mubia,*" meaning "there are no marked differences between a European missionary and the settler/colonizer" (Gathogo 2008). Such fear and mistrust were huge setbacks to the young Digo mission. In 1912 and 1913, the Digo mission was temporarily abandoned.

Although there were attempts by another CMS missionary, Rev. George Wright, to revive the Digo mission in 1914, it did not rise to the expectations, particularly when compared with neighboring CMS missions. It is only in 1975, when the first African clergy from Digo land was ordained as an Anglican priest, Ven. Canon Elijah Kubeta Ramtu that work was restored in Digo land. Ten years later, Simon Pore Maneno was ordained as the second Anglican clergyman (1985) from Digo land. As noted in Gathogo (2013), the overall Anglican influence in Kenya spread fast from 1844 to 1930. In particular, various Anglican missions had managed to by-pass Digo land despite its being a "stone's throw" from Rabai where the first Anglican mission was inaugurated by the pioneer missionary, Ludwig Krapf. In particular, the various Anglican missions had managed to penetrate the interior of East Africa with gusto to the extent that some interior mission trainees returned from Nairobi to Mombasa to reengineer the Digo mission first with Rev. Bans, and later with Rev. George Wright. Indeed, there were well-established mission stations besides Digo land that had both local and European missionary input, on the East Coast of Africa as early as 1844 in the case of Mombasa (Leven House), Freretown (1875), Sagalla (1883), Jilore (1890), Mbale (1900), Kaloleni (1904) and others. In the central and western parts of Kenya, there were well established mission stations such as Kabete (1900), Weithaga (1904), Wusi (1905), Kahuhia (1906), Nairobi (1906), Maseno (1906), Kisumu (1909), Kabare (1910), Kigari (1910), Mutira (1912), Butere (1912), Gathukeine (1913), Ng'iya (1921), Kacheliba (1929), and Marsabit (1930).

In the rest of East Africa, namely: Uganda, Burundi, Rwanda and then Tanganyika (now Tanzania), more CMS missions were founded as well. Such missions include: Baganda (1876-77), Moshi (1878), Rwanda (1916-19), and Burundi (1934). Additionally, the Universities' Mission to Central Africa (UMCA or the Anglo-Catholic, also called high Anglican) and the Church Missionary Society (CMS, the evangelical Anglican, also called the low Anglican) began their discourses in 1864 to 1878 at Mpwapwa, Tanzania. While the various missions in eastern Africa went on to demonstrate Christ's three-fold ministry of healing (by establishing dispensaries), teaching (by establishing schools), and evangelism (by establishing churches), the Digo mission continued to lag behind. Was there any light at the end of the tunnel? Certainly, the ordination of Ven. Canon Elijah Ramtu, as the first indigenous clergyman in 1975 and Rev. Simon Maneno Pore in 1985 did not really help matters, as more was expected from this mission in close proximity to the pioneer Rabai mission centre, which ought to have placed it in an advantaged position.

Coercion in the Digo Mission

Another setback that confronted the Mijikenda mission, inclusive of the Digo mission, was coercion by anti-Christian crusaders, particularly from the religious traditionalists and Muslim Arabs. In the mission's initial stage, it encountered a major setback when six Christian virgins were forcefully buried alive in the full glare of the public in present day Changamwe District of Mombasa County, at a place called Bahati, near the present day Changamwe roundabout in 1912 (Ramtu 2018). Since 1902, when the British established their rule of law in Mombasa, which superseded the Sharia law, it was never easy for the Sultan of Zanzibar's appointees (*Liwalis*). Just as his son Ali had became a *Liwali* of Mombasa, Salim, had no alternative but to cooperate with the British administrators and missionaries who had greatly increased in number, and who meddled with the local administration. The British were not only pushing for the abolishment of the slave trade and the emancipation of slaves, but some missionaries were allegedly "buying off" freedom for some African slaves. Salim's successor, his son Ali, was even accused of being a British puppet by his Arab-Islamic constituency. As a result, tensions mounted which eventually saw the burial of the six Christian virgins of African descent.

Like the Vestal Virgins (*Vestālēs*) in the state religion of ancient Rome, who were stoned to death or whipped to death upon being caught in sexual transgressions, the six Mombasa African Christian virgins met their unwarranted death in a weird and bizarre way. Considering that they were not guilty of any charge, save for the fear that they could have joined the new wave of European missionaries, their untimely persecution was totally misplaced. In the case of the Vestal Virgins of ancient Rome, the fifth King of Rome, Tarquinius Priscus who reigned between 616 to 579 BCE/BC, added an even heavier punishment when he decided that a guilty Vestal Virgin (*Vestālis*) should be buried alive (Chisholm, 1911). Ironically, no one was allowed to shed the blood of any of these Vestal Virgins (*Vestālēs*) hence the reason why Tarquinius Priscus introduced the idea of burying Vestal Virgins alive. Before the drama of burying the six virgins on the East African coast, there were fears of Arab cruelty all over the region. A Kenyan international motivational speaker and a lawyer, Patrick Loch Otieno Lumumba, has been quoted as saying that the first people to capture and take African men out of the continent to the outside world were the Arabs. According to this theory, African men were castrated immediately after they stepped out of Africa so as to avoid further procreation of the black race. While concrete evidence is yet to be found of this practice, the fears, rumors, and memories of such brutalities had a profound effect on Protestant missions on the East African coast, and in Digo land in particular.

In the Changamwe case, the ritualistic burial of the six healthy virgins resulted in the establishment of a centre for teaching Islamic education (*madrass*) on the same spot (Ramtu, 2018). This took place after the CMS missions appeared to be making inroads in the Muslim dominated areas of the East African coast. This ritual act was inspired by the earlier murder of the first Bishop of Equatorial Africa, James Hannington, by Kabaka Mwanga of Baganda as he entered Uganda from the east in 1885. This violent and inhumane act was meant to send a warning signal that Christianity would not gain a foothold in the coastal region of Kenya of which Digo land is a part. Ironically, this dramatic episode scared the European missionaries who feared the emergence of a Muslim-Christian war akin to the Crusades (otherwise called the Christian Holy Wars) that took place of the 11th century CE/AD. Indeed, this was the sad moment when the Latin Church turned their guns on the Muslim "intruders" in their so-called territories, and scored victory in the first Crusade that took place in 1095. In other words, the "Christian armies" from Western Europe obeyed Pope Urban II's plea to go to war against the Muslim forces in the Holy Land. Interestingly, the first Crusade secured Jerusalem from the Muslims. With the East Coast of Africa having been a battlefield since the Arab-Portuguese wars of the 16th and 17th centuries and even before this, the 19th century CMS missionaries were not willing to pursue that route.

In the case of the Changamwe virgins, the public burial was ironically witnessed by one of the sons of the prominent Arab leaders of Mombasa, Sir Ali bin Salim al-Busaidi (1870-1940). In turn, the then *Liwali* of Mombasa, Ali bin Salim was a prominent Arab figure, a member of the Al-Busaidi family that ruled East Africa in the 19th century. Ali was knighted by King George of England for his contribution during the First World War (1914-18) and at the beginning of the Second World War in 1939. His father, Salim bin Khalfan, served as *Liwali* or Governor of Mombasa during the introduction of British colonial rule. Khalfan had been appointed as *Liwali* (Governor) of Mombasa by the Sultan of Zanzibar in the 1880s. This was before the Imperial British East Africa (IBEA) Company under William Mackinnon (1823-1893) established its headquarters in Mombasa in 1887. His son, Ali bin Salim, took the mantle of leadership after his death in the early part of the 20th century. Sir Ali al-Busaidi fought for Arab rights in the British Kenyan colony and worked hard to establish the first Arab school and a library called Seif Bin Salem at Mombasa in 1912, which is now the Kenya National Library on the Island. He also founded another school in Malindi.

Although Sir Ali Bin Salim was not necessarily privy to the public burial of the six virgins, one of his sons sneaked out and witnessed these bizarre rituals that were meant to stop the further growth of Christianity. He became very upset and was eventually traumatized. After these events, he ran away from his Islamic home and joined the church where he was baptized as Henry Right at the Mombasa Memorial Cathedral. While the religious "traditionalists" did not make similar rituals to stop Islam, which had already gained roots in the coastal region, they were also explicit that Christianity was not welcome. It was too legalistic, as opposed to Islam, which did not appear keen to fight off cultural elements such as polygamy. Interestingly, these rituals appeared to have scared Digo land more than other any other coastal area. Although the leading ritualists were not necessarily from Digo land, the effects of such rituals were clearly felt across the region.

Generally, the larger Mijikenda community showed only slow Christian growth as they all held strongly to certain cultural elements that were communally important. In particular, the Digo expected a person who had undergone a misfortune to undertake cultural rituals that were communally conducted and which could ironically hurt the person who was already injured. Equally, marriage negotiations required one to give out beer, and the residues of beer (*sira*). In turn, *sira* had to be "read" by an "expert" who would interpret the meaning. Such ritualistic collectivism eventually interfered with individual choice, and in a sense "criminalized" individual choice. To be on the "right side," one had to go with the societal interests rather than make a decision as an individual. While this is typically part of our African heritage in general, the extremity of the matter appears to hurt the natural dynamism of any given culture the world over. The ripple effect was that conversion to Christianity in Digo land had to await collective approval, which has taken a long time despite the modern generation appearing to be less tied to such cultural collectivism. As globalization rules the world in the 21st century, individual choice will certainly gain more of a foothold in our communalistic Africa, and in Digo land in particular.

Beliefs in Witchcraft

One major challenge in the Digo mission is the belief in witchcraft. In our conversations with Digo elders in October of 2018, I noted that there are bloodcurdling stories related to witchcraft that scare off people from engaging with the Christian faith and other forms of progressive development. In particular, we could hear a "recent" episode where a person was allegedly circumcised at night by unknown people, only to notice it in the morning. Such beliefs in evil supernatural forces that can destroy a person who converts to another religion, or progresses in another way which tend to retard general growth. Research done by an American professor, Boris Gershman, has shown that belief in witchcraft takes its toll on the economy. It erodes social capital – "the trusting and co-operative networks between people on which businesses rely" (Bolton 2018: 1). It builds the notion that people can send curses that cause bad things to happen to other people. In his research on some areas of sub-Saharan Africa, Gershman found a "robust negative association" (Bolton 2018: 1) between witchcraft beliefs and trust. Certainly, the belief in witchcraft also causes familial or societal tensions, suspicions, hatred, violence, and at its worst death. In the coastal region of Kenya, where the Digo mission is located, we find many cases of mob killings of suspected witches by impatient youths. To this end, Gershman urges us to invest in what he calls "greater education in the realities of witchcraft" in order to help foster improved trust, which will eventually help economies to grow. He says that education may contribute to an environment with higher levels of trust and mutual assistance, "insofar as it helps to promote a rational worldview and reduce the attribution of any misfortune in life to the supernatural evil forces of other people in the community" (Bolton 2018: 1).

Loyalty to the Ancestral Pantheons

Another major impediment to the Digo mission is strong "loyalty" to the traditional religion, a phenomenon where cultural practices are too sacred to be doubted, questioned, and/or debated. Through cultural debates, a "what if" view is critical as it helps us to explore the dynamism of culture. Considering that no culture is either perfect or static, cultural loyalty need not be an impediment to other progressive ideas. It was saddening to hear from some Digo elders whom we interviewed, that even after being educated, most people revert to the Digo culture, some of which is not friendly to the Gospel of Christ. As John Baur (1994) has noted, all of the nine sub-groups of the larger Mijikenda communities, part of whom are the Digo, had an exceptional attachment to their traditional religion. Only the Digo and one quarter of the Duruma had accepted Islam. The other eight sub-groups that form the Mijikenda community stuck to their ancestral pantheons. As Baur (1994: 228) says of the Digo's cousins, the Giriama,

> They had their sacred villages of selected elders who ruled the whole society. In their own schools, their children were given instruction in [African] religion, morals and cattle rearing. They were convinced that their traditions had served them well and saw no need for a new religion. So, when in 1904 the Holy Ghost Fathers opened their Giriama Mission with children from Bagamoyo

[Tanzania], hardly a child from the surroundings came to join the classes, and the Precious Blood Sisters even had to close their girls' school after a few years.

Late Translation of the Chidigo Bible

Another critical challenge in the Digo mission is the late translation of the Bible into the Chidigo language. The entire New Testament was translated into Chidigo in 2005, which doesn't help matters as this is relatively recent. This however needs to be followed with literacy training so as to help people read the Bible for themselves and keep the word in their hearts. Undoubtedly, a full translation of the entire Bible needs to be prioritized by the relevant policy makers. Apart from literacy training, it is critically important that as many sons and daughters as possible from Digo land be encouraged to enroll at the local Bishop Hannington Institute - College of Theology and Development, Pwani International Christian College, St Paul's University, Daystar University, and Kenya Methodist University among other institutions, and be prepared for ministerial training. To this effect, a local and international campaign should be championed through the diverse avenues created by breakthroughs in science and technology. Certainly, it will be encouraging to see more and more theologically prepared local Digo pastors ministering in the Chidigo dialect, and using both Old and New Testaments in the Chidigo language. In considering that language is the major vehicle of communication and culture, the Digo mission will have a guaranteed future when approached from this perspective.

The Poverty Concern

In addressing poverty as a key challenge in the Digo mission, as our interviews with local elders on October 9 and 10, 2018 showed, we must appreciate a broad understanding of poverty, its dimensions and manifestations, and indeed focus on how to overcome it. If it affects Christian missions, then Christians must devise several ways of nipping it in the bud. Primarily, we were told that the Digo people joined the trading Arabs back in the seventh century. As they traded, the Digo were eventually converted to the Islamic faith. In the hope of improving their lot, they unilaterally embraced the Islamic faith; and while Islam gained heavily, poverty did not end with this conversion. It is still a challenge right into the 21st century.

In attempting to define poverty, it is worthwhile to reason with J. D. Jones (1990: 94) who contends that modern poverty research begins with the work of Charles Booth and Seebohm Rowntree who, at the end of the 19th century, "provided the first systematic discussion of poverty founded on modern scientific analysis." These two gentlemen developed subsistence definitions of poverty and they viewed the poor primarily as those who were just able or even unable to provide for their physical subsistence. This is certainly a limiting definition as poverty can also be spiritual, psychological, and/or material lack among other dimensions.

In analysing the nature of poverty, Bryant Myers (1999) gives five descriptions of poverty, which is first of all a deficit. Secondly, he examines Robert Chambers' view of poverty as entanglement. In that connection, Chambers sees poverty in terms of material lack, physical weakness eg. due to poor health, isolation e.g., from roads, vulnerability, say, due to cultural demands such as dowry and powerlessness e.g., lack of ability to influence life around a person. Myers (1999) adds a sixth dimension to complete Chambers view which is a spiritual poverty. By spiritual poverty, he meant, "dysfunctional relationships with God, each other, the community and creation" (Myers 1999: 67). As he says, "they may lack hope and be unable to believe that change is possible. They may never have heard the gospel…" (Myers 1999: 67). Thirdly, Myers (1999) quotes John Friedman who sees poverty as lack of social organisation and lack of access to the political process. Fourthly, he quotes Jayakumar Christian who sees poverty as disempowerment. This disempowerment can be in the form of a culture system, social, personal, biophysical, or a religious system. Fifthly, he quotes Ravi Jayakaran who sees poverty as a lack of freedom to grow (Myers 1999).

Diagram on Dimensions of Poverty

	Type of Poverty	Causes
1	Terminal	Describes those who are poor both at the beginning and the end of their lives.
2	Endemic	Caused by low productivity and a poor resource base. It is reflected by low income, poor nutrition and health, often affecting small holders on rain-fed farmlands, small-scale fishermen and herders.
3	Overcrowding	In this type of poverty, population is heavily concentrated into areas of high density, for instance Ruanda or Maragoli.
4	Inherited	In the case of inherited poverty, poor parents pass on their poverty to their children. In other words, it is an unending cycle of poverty.
5	Temporary	This is caused by some of the same hazards as in the case of Instant Poverty. This however lasts for a shorter period. An example can be rain comes suddenly, loans are obtained, war ceases.
6	Instant	This may refer to sudden hazards and circumstances like earthquakes, typhoons, and tsunami, drought, bankruptcy, war and refugee movements.
7	Relative	Refers to deprivation of opportunities, where material assets and self-respect are regarded as normal in the community to which people belong. An example is: people may be adequately fed and basically housed, but lack material possessions, educational opportunities, and so on.
8	Absolute	Refers to deprivation of elements necessary to sustain life and health, such as adequate food, safe drinking water, shelter, land, employment and personal security. Sadly, the absolute poor are more likely to keep on returning to a state of poverty despite improvements in society, such as better market conditions.

9	Hidden	Hidden poverty can be similar to relative poverty in that people may have adequate food and shelter, but lack other basic needs. Such basic needs may include sufficient heat in cold weather or access to health care, and yet they do not report such needs. Additionally, deprivation of remote populations may be hidden.
10	New	This new form of poverty comes when income and savings of workers and pensioners are eroded by high unemployment, inflation rates, or where small cash-crop farmers are ruined by high input costs and low prices of agricultural products.

The theme of poverty is critical in the mission of the church in the 21st century. John Stott defines mission as everything that the church is sent to do (cited in Gathogo 2011b), hence the reason to understand the Digo mission from a broader dimension. Indeed, poverty is a missiological concern, as it doesn't manifest the kingdom of God. Certainly, when we see masses of people walking through the valleys of death, we become concerned and wonder: Who is to blame? Why does the situation happen? Is poverty an impediment to God's mission in Digo land and the rest of tropical Africa? And how best can we address this huge issue?

After an interview with the leading cleric from Digo land (Ven. Canon Elijah Kubeta Ramtu 2018), it came out clearly that poverty is the one single factor that has perpetually hindered the progress in the Digo mission. According to Ramtu (2018), poverty constitutes 75% of the challenges of the Digo mission. As modern Christian missionaries, the pastors in particular, move out to propound the message of Christ to a society that is predominantly characterized by Islamic and traditional faiths, they lack something to use in order to attract more people to Christianity, such as films, foods, compelling literature, and so on.

Learning from Thomas Kalume

In my research on Thomas Kuto Kalume, a cleric-turned-politician (done with Rev. Alphonce Mwaro Baya, now Bishop, in 2015), entitled: "Ecclesiastical and Political Leaderships in One Armpit: Reconstructing the Memory of Thomas Kalume" (Gathogo 2015), we noted that Rev.

Kalume lost his Malindi North (now Magarini) parliamentary seat in 1974 when he refused to give his constituents monetary hand-outs. Kalume's wisdom of showing people how to produce food rather than dishing out relief food to them did not sink down to the people, as the Giriama who are ethnic cousins of the Digo still rejected him, and eventually voted him out of parliament.

Thus, as Kalume sought reelection during the December 1974 general elections, he was weighed down by his understanding of real development as empowerment, which was not well understood by the voters. Like President Nyerere of Tanzania, Kalume held that the better way of feeding a hungry person is not to give him fish but to show the person how to fish (Gathogo 2011a). It is for this reason that he sought to avoid giving monetary hand-outs to his poverty-stricken constituents, but instead sought to empower people through the building of schools, liaising with the national government to provide infrastructure, and so on.

When his constituents went into his office to seek financial hand-outs so as to pay fees for their children, Kalume would lecture them about how to manage their few resources prudently and avoid relying on relief food, donors, or handouts from individual rich people. He would also advise them to sell part of their livestock and/or farm produce. This refusal to give handouts was meant to empower them and thereby make them see their huge potential, and indeed their many assets. The ripple effect he hoped for was that they would avoid focusing on deficiencies rather than assets. In this, Kalume hoped, he would kill the dependency syndrome in the society. Unfortunately, this made him unpopular with a section of his constituents who saw the legislator's role as that of "a weekend donor." Like the proverbial kicks from a thankless donkey, they sent him home in December 1974.

In putting too much emphasis on education, and in his rejection of humanitarian handouts and eventually opting for increased productivity and astute management of resources, Kalume was vouching for sustainable development, which are indeed critical elements in the 21st century models of growth and prosperity. If Africa were to follow Kalume's path, the reward would be immense. Certainly, Kalume could see the distinction between development and relief as in the diagram below:

	Development	Relief
1	Is long-term	Is short-term
2	Solves ongoing constant problems	Solves an emergency situation
3	Helps people become self-sufficient	Tends to build dependency
4	Builds people as well as economic health	Usually not concerned with training, educating, empowering, or growth
5	Involves the people as participants and contributors	Sees people as recipients, not participants
6	Meets felt needs	Meets presumed needs
7	Has a multi-sector approach	Addresses single problems
8	Is insider controlled	Is outsider controlled

In this understanding, Kalume understood relief as nothing but doing something for someone who cannot do it for himself or herself. It is a crisis intervention, an attempt to provide some form of assistance that will aid the individual or group to return to a prior condition. To an extent, intervention is needed to effect a rescue, but cannot remain perpetually. On the other hand, Kalume understood development as that which assists people in effectively addressing their own concerns: fix their own sewers, fix their huge gaping holes without feeling inadequate or expecting someone else to solve their own problems. He knew that genuine development is seen when ordinary people are philosophically and intellectually empowered to appreciate that they are masters and servants of their respective destinies. Indeed, development assumes that people have the innate skills and abilities to take charge of their lives, while at the same time acknowledging the need for facilitators to provide an example, instruction, and access to needed resources. In view of this, Kalume looked forward to genuine development that brings people together and eventually keeps them working together rather than begging from one another, or perpetually begging from the few more well-endowed members of the society. Kalume, the second Anglican cleric after John Mbiti to graduate with a theological degree, has huge lessons for the Digo mission and for tropical Africa in general.

Conclusion

The chapter began by attempting to locate the Digo as one of the nine sub-groups that form the Mijikenda community. This chapter has journeyed with the challenges and setbacks that have driven the Digo mission to its lowest ebb. In a country like Kenya, where Christians in general constitute 83% of the population, with Protestants at 47.7%, Catholics at 23.4%, other Christians at 11.9% and with the Muslim population standing at 11.2%, traditionalists at 1.7%, others at 1.6%, agnostics (neutralists) at 2.4%, and unspecified at 0.2%, the Digo land figures stand apart (Joshuah 2018). It is in Kwale County, the Digo homeland, where Muslims in the 21st century stand at 79% and traditionalists at 20%, which makes an interesting case study. Why does this situation appear unique? This chapter has surveyed, though not exhaustively, some of the key setbacks that have compounded the Digo mission since 1844. Such setbacks include, blind adherence to ancestral pantheons, the history of Islamic civilization and trade with the east coast, coercion by the anti-Christ, poverty, late Chidigo Bible translation, a culture of dependency amidst plenty, and beliefs in witchcraft among other concerns. Although poor stewardship and leadership are not discussed in this chapter, they are well implied in the discourses therein. As Africa begs for transformative leadership that goes beyond mere servanthood and beyond transactional maintenance of the status quo, but empowers everyone to find the solution and work for the common and individual good, the Digo mission needs to be given more attention. In adhering to the 21st century skills movement, this chapter has methodically employed problem-solving techniques, critical thinking, embraced science and technology, employed the 3Rs of professionalism (responsibility, respect, and risk-taking), and more importantly, expressed a passion for the subject at hand. The Digo mission is certainly a mission in need of our attention.

Chapter 12

Global Team Mission in Digo Land
Rev. Josephat J. Murutu

Introduction

This chapter is to find out about the existing relationship between Anglican Diocese of Mombasa and Global Teams-Kenya (GT-K) and see how the two can partner in mission for the propagation of the Gospel in the Diocese of Mombasa. The Ven. Dr. Bryson Samboja, who is the Archdeacon of Matuga, is an Anglican priest but he is also the Director of Global Teams-Africa, Kenya being a part of this work. He has seven churches which are referred to as Emmanuel Community Churches (ECC), but are not Anglican, and are being served by ten pastors who are also not Anglicans. He also has started a school with more than one hundred and forty-five (145) pupils, and is also very independent from the diocese of Mombasa where he serves as an Archdeacon. He remits his statutory deductions to the diocese for transmission onward but does not receive a salary from the Diocese.

How did Global Teams Come to be?

Dr. Samboja went to America for further mission studies. During this period of study, he had a calling from God to come back after his studies and reach out to the Digo community on the coast. This community is largely Muslim and only a few of the clans are Christian. He made an official launch of his mission and ministry at the ACK guest house in the presence of two bishops; Rt. Rev. Dr. Samson Mwaluda, then bishop of Taita Taveta and Rt. Rev. Julius R.K. Kalu, then bishop of Mombasa commissioning this work with the witness of several clergy from both dioceses. After this launch, the Ven. Dr. Samboja was left on his own to navigate the terrains of Digo land with no financial support from the dioceses except for his dog collar and ordination license (Samboja's report from the leaders meeting in June 2018).

History

Global Teams was formed in 1983 under the name Episcopal World Mission (EWM) by mission-minded Episcopalians who organized a "faith mission" sending agency. There was no official denominational or financial link with the national Episcopal Church or any other denominational body. However, all of the original Board Members and missionaries were Episcopalian.

The original focus was to recruit and send Episcopalians to work under existing worldwide Anglican churches. The missionaries sent during this time were Bible teachers, evangelists, administrative support for local leadership, and medical personnel. Projects were started including orphanages, training centers, and clinics.

In 1993, the Executive Board broadened the vision of the organization to include a focus on unreached people groups and sending non-Episcopalian missionaries. By 2003 EWM had grown to include missionaries serving in or coming from 19 countries. The missionaries were predominantly, but not exclusively, Episcopalian. In addition, the thrust of their missionary work began to focus on two major efforts:

1. Raising up missionaries *from* many nations around the world to work together in multi-cultural teams.

2. Placing teams *among* people groups least reached by the Gospel in order to start new movements of believers, small groups, and churches.

One result of this new focus was that EWM's missionary force also became increasingly multi-national. By 2003, their missionaries came from New Zealand, (Laos Rmove), Costa Rica, Korea, Kenya,

Canada, the UK, and North America. Recruitment was actively taking place in other African, Asian, and Latin American countries as well.

Because of the growth of EWM as an international mission, the name was changed in 2002 to EWM-Global Teams, and to Global Teams as of January, 2004. This also reflects their increasing emphasis on team-based ministry.

Their missionaries have been used by God to initiate new people movements among unreached people groups in several contexts. There is new work beginning in over a dozen more unreached people groups. Global Teams receives no denominational funding but depends solely upon the financial partnership of individuals and churches for its support.

Mission

- Global Teams equips and sends field partners from many nations to multiply disciples of Jesus Christ within cultures least familiar with the Gospel.

Vision:

- To see the heart of Christ in the skin of every culture.

Global Teams' Statement of Faith

- Global Teams affirms that our purpose is to obey the Great Commission of our Lord, Jesus Christ.
- We affirm our belief in historic Christianity as revealed in the Scriptures and summarized in The Apostles' Creed and The Nicene Creed.
- We recognize the need today for reaffirming the following beliefs and articulating them within the forms of expression and vocabulary suitable to new cultural contexts.
  - **The Holy Trinity**
    The mystery of the Holy Trinity, namely, that the one God exists eternally in three persons: Father, Son and Holy Spirit; and has so revealed himself to us in the Gospel.

- **The Lord Jesus Christ**
  The full deity and full humanity of our Lord Jesus Christ, God Incarnate, who by reason of His birth of the Virgin Mary, sinless life, atoning death, bodily resurrection, glorious ascension and triumphant reign, is the only mediator between God and man.
- **The Holy Scriptures**
  The trustworthiness of the canonical books of the Old and New Testaments as "God's word written" which contain all things necessary for salvation, teach God's will for His world, and have supreme authority for faith, life and continuous renewal and reform of the Church.
- **Justification and Sanctification**
  The justification of the repenting and believing sinner as God's gracious act of declaring them righteous on the ground of the reconciling death of Christ, who suffered in our place and rose again for us; and sanctification as the gracious continuing activity of the Holy Spirit in the justified believer, perfecting their repentance, nurturing the new life implanted in them, transforming them into Christ's image, and enabling them to do good works in the world.
- **The Christian Church**
  The Church as the Body of Christ, whose members belong to the new Kingdom of God, and are called to live in the world in the power of the Spirit, worshiping God confessing His truth, proclaiming Christ, supporting one another in love, and giving themselves in sacrificial service to those in need. Forms of organization and fellowship will, and should, vary according to cultural contexts.
- **Spiritual Gifts and Ministry**
  The calling of all Christians to exercise their God-given gifts in ministry, and to work, witness, and suffer for Christ; together with the particular calling of ordained ministers who, by preaching, teaching, and pastoral care, are to train and equip God's people for His service, and to present them mature in Christ.

- **Gospel Sacraments**
  The sacraments of Baptism and Holy Communion as "visible signs" which proclaim the Gospel, and are a means of grace by which faith is quickened and strengthened. In particular, the significance of the Lord's Supper as a communion in the Body and Blood of Christ, who offers Himself to us in the action of this sacrament, so that by faith we may feed on Him in our hearts and offer ourselves to Him in gratitude for our salvation through His cross. Also, the openness of the Lord's Table as the place where all baptized believers, being one in Christ, are free to celebrate their common salvation in the Lord, and express the common devotion to His person and His service.
- **The Return of Christ**
  The personal return in glory of our Lord Jesus Christ at the end of this age for the resurrection of the dead (some to life, some to condemnation); for the glorification of His church, and for the renewal of the whole creation.

Activities:

Global Teams is an international mission movement focused on reaching the 6,648 unreached people groups. Put another way, their desire is to reach the 2.9 billion people who have never heard the gospel. Following John 1:14.

Church Planting Through Global Teams

Global Teams is presently engaged with 166 unreached people groups worldwide, helping to plant churches within the culture of these groups. When planting churches, Global Teams follows the model of John 1:14: "The Word became flesh and made his dwelling among us."

As a result of this approach, church planting movements emerge in forms and expressions that fit the culture of a people group and enable the Gospel to expand like yeast in the dough. Twenty-nine (29) of these movements have emerged among Muslims, Hindus, Buddhists, and animists.

Local Leadership

Believers who "remain" are leaders from the beginning. Just as we see in the Gospels and Acts, existing local leadership is mentored right away, preserving societal leadership patterns. This allows the natural and spiritual gifts of the body to emerge and lead the church.

Liturgical Worship

Worship forms for these new church plants are developed through the careful study of scripture. In order for the emerging movement to be seen as one from within its own culture, new believers, through the careful study of scripture, develop worship forms which allow the emerging church planting movement to continue to identify with its own culture and people group.

Bible Translations

The Word of God is translated into the local language as needed for these new church planting movements. When oral and written translations are undertaken, they are carefully researched and meticulously checked so that the integrity of God's Word is kept and shared within this culture. This work is done by multi-national translation teams, including translators from that culture.

Locally-Sustained Churches

The new church plants are independent and locally sustained. Emerging church planting movements develop ways to support their movement, evangelize, choose new leaders and discover the truth of God's Word.

Global Mission Fields to Unreached People Groups

Founded as a Christian missionary agency in 1983, Global Teams recognized in the year 2000 that its mission is to work with unreached people groups throughout the world who have not yet heard the Gospel of

Christ. They have accomplished this through multi-national missionary teams from Africa, North America, Latin America, and Asia.

Global Teams reaches people for Christ right where they find them. God ordained the nations into which all people are born, therefore they honor people and learn how they think, live, work, and play.

Their international missionary teams are sent from training bases around the world to live and work among unreached people groups. They have grown to over 466 missionaries (or field partners) sent from all over the world working in 39 different countries, with 166 unreached people groups who are hearing the Gospel for the first time. Through their missionary work, 29 movements to Jesus have emerged among Muslims, Hindus, Buddhists, and animists. In just two of these groups, over 13,000 house churches have been planted across the globe.

Still so Much Work to be Done

There are still so many people to reach in the world with the Gospel. In fact, according to IMG.org, there are 121,274,620 unreached people throughout the world who have not yet heard the good news of Christ. That means there is still a lot of work to be done and a lot of seeds to be sown by multi-cultural missionaries or field partners. They have no problem learning more about how others can make a difference.

Because of this great need, Global Teams has become globally involved in producing Bible translations as well as training and coordinating translation personnel and projects.

The aim of Global Teams' Bible translation ministries is best summarized as: the production of accurate and appropriate communication of the scriptures through written and oral translations of the Old and New Testaments, hand in hand with the active promotion of obedient engagement with the scriptures during and following the translation process. Therefore, four key terms shape their understanding of translation: authority, accuracy, appropriateness, and audience.

Authority & Accuracy

Along with the wider community of Bible translation agencies, "They affirm the inspiration and authority of the Holy Scriptures and commit themselves to translate the scriptures accurately, without loss, change, distortion, or embellishment of the meaning of the original text. Accuracy in Bible translation is the faithful communication, as exactly as possible, of that meaning, determined according to sound principles of exegesis." (Cited from the *Forum of Bible Agencies International*, statement #11)

Their commitment to accuracy in translation flows from their deep trust in the authority of the scriptures. They recognize that the authoritative message of the scriptures is most fully embraced, obeyed, and understood when accurate translation is also culturally appropriate. This goal of accurate and appropriate communication requires careful analysis of the specific linguistic, cultural, and religious factors that may cause potential misunderstandings or misinterpretations of the biblical text. All translation personnel, and the translation consultants who advise them, are trained to identify these factors and work with translation teams as they seek to express the meaning of the biblical text and key terms in the clearest way possible.

Appropriateness & Audience

The cultural and linguistic contexts in which the Bible is being translated around the world are very diverse. Therefore, the specific cultural and linguistic factors of each situation may cause some aspects of certain translations to look very different in different contexts in order to actually communicate the same meaning of the biblical text faithfully to the respective audiences.

The audience does not determine the meaning of the message, but how the audience understands their initial drafts and samples will shape how they edit and change a translation. That's to ensure that it communicates accurately in an appropriate way so as to minimize the misunderstanding and misapplication of the biblical message as much as possible.

Rigorous Checks in the Context of Actual Usage

In order to achieve the most accurate and appropriate translations humanly possible, every translation project goes through a number of stages in which there are rigorous checks and revisions by the team and by the consultants who work with them. Whenever possible, this checking and revision is done in the context of actual usage of the scriptures in inductive bible studies, evangelistic storying, reproduction of churches, and development of leaders. At the same time, they ultimately rely upon the reality and ongoing work of God's Spirit to change hearts, renew minds, and continually transform those who seek to hear and obey the scriptures.

Bryson and his wife, Deborah, desired to reach an unreached people group with the word of God and train other Kenyans to do the same.

Says Bryson:

> I am an ordained minister in the Anglican Church of Kenya. I have served in a diocese in Kenya since 1984, nine years of which I served as the principal of Bishop Hannington Institute, preparing ordinands for full-time ministry. My Christian mission began in 1972, soon after I gave my life to Christ. My new experience in Christ changed my inner being; shaping my values, attitudes, and motives. I knew I had a vocation to fulfill; serving my Lord. I was led to a life of prayer and fasting. I became fully involved in the Christian Union at my school, including leading services and preaching. Later I had a call to serve as a full-time minister in the Church, so I joined the ordained ministry. In 2002, while studying in the United States, I learned about Global Teams. I discovered that Global Teams had the same vision as I did so I joined them as a field partner. In 2006, my studies were completed and my wife and I went back to Kenya and started our ministry with an unreached people group.

Samboja further states that God gave them a great dream which they followed after five years to resolve that God was leading them into a ministry that would "revolve around spiritual guidance, education, health, farming, and social welfare." Guided by the vision he had in a dream, Samboja went ahead to implement the mission at Kwale of which he says:

> On one and a quarter acres of land that God provided, we have been able to construct buildings that serve as a primary school during the week days and a place of worship on Sundays. We have over 145 children enrolled in pre-school through 8th grade. We have built a number of other churches in the years since and are seeing many people come to faith in Jesus Christ. We thank God for the good quality education we are providing to these children. With your prayers and assistance, this community will be able to experience the love of Christ and lead a better life.

Lavington United Church

Besides new types of mission, the Anglican Church has also been involved in new inorative and ecumenical ways of building churches, like this example from Nairobi: Lavington United Church was fo9unded in 1960 through a joint effort by the Anglican Church of Kenya (ACK), Methodist Church of Kenya (MCK), and the Presbyterian Church of East Africa (PCEA) as a community church to minister to the Lavington community.

> In the calm of the post-World War II 1950's, a number of people felt they wanted a change and many chose Africa as a sparsely populated, "and of opportunity". Nairobi in particular expanded rapidly with an influx of settlers from overseas – mainly from Europe, but also local Africans. In the new housing estates around Nairobi, groups of Christians began meeting in the spirit of "where two or three are gathered in My Name I am there with them" (Matthew 18:20). They were

galvanized into action by the offer of two free plots from the Buchannan's Kenya Estates, makers of a well-known Scottish Black and White whiskey, who were developing the Lavington area. One plot was to be for the Anglicans and one for the Presbyterians (there were few Methodists in Nairobi at that time).

Inspired by the Holy Spirit and encouraged by the shortage of manpower, money, and other resources, representatives of the three mainline protestant churches – Anglican, Presbyterian and Methodist decided to join together and use one of the plots for a combined united church and the other for a minister's house and church hall. The Methodists provided the largest sum of money and a minister, so it was decided that the church should be under the jurisdiction and discipline of the Methodist Church in Kenya. So, a delicate balance had to be struck by the Leaders of Lavington Church between being a normal Methodist church and one that catered to the Anglicans, Presbyterians, and the Community of Lavington in general.

Truly God led those early leaders and congregations as they signed a formal agreement to build a united church and Lavington Church was formally opened by the Governor Sir Patrick Renison on June 4, 1960. Some members of Lavington doubted whether such an ecumenical arrangement would work in practice. But July 4, 2010 we celebrated the 50th (Golden) Anniversary, so it is clear that with God all things are possible.[1]

The future of the church in Digo land depends in large part to the use of innovative new ways of reaching people. Lavington United Church and Global Teams are just two possible examples the church might follow in extending greater outreach into Digo land.

---

[1] Material on Lavington United church taken from an article by the Late Dr. Andrew Hicks who went to be with the Lord in May 2017 at the advanced age of 98. He witnessed the laying of the foundations of the church in 1959. (http://www.lavingtonunited.org/index.php/about-luc/our-history)

Chapter 13

Conclusion: What Can World Christianity Learn From Kwale County?

Robert A. Danielson

The preface to this book puts forward the essential question it is attempting to answer. After 114 years of Anglican missions in Digo land, only 1% of the population is Christian. What has gone wrong? Various essays examine cultural, social, religious, and historical issues to find potential answers to this question, as well as offering insights into future mission projects. The answer is important to help guide the Anglican Church into how it might more effectively evangelize this region of Kenya. But as an outsider, I have a slightly different question to answer. How can missiology in other parts of the world learn from this serious attempt to understand the history of mission in Digo land?

The essays in this book are a fascinating exploration of a new kind of history, one that is not defined by traditional Western standards of historical resources. In terms of modern missiology we desperately need histories, such as this one, to fill a number of crucial gaps in our knowledge of the mission of the Church. Traditionally, Western scholars, utilizing archives and publications produced by the missionaries, have written mission histories, and in the process this has often left the people who were the subject of the missionary outreach voiceless. In the case of this book, history is arising from the missionized, especially in the creative use of oral interviews of Church elders from among the Digo people.

Such an approach does raise some crucial questions for traditional mission historians and trained archivists, such as myself. How do we evaluate this type of history? How do we use oral history in conjunction with traditional historical approaches? How do we avoid favoring one type of history over another to reach a more complete understanding of mission history? These are just a few important questions raised by a book like this.

Comparing Traditional and Oral History

Perhaps as a comparison, it is interesting to examine an article by Dickson K. Nkonge, entitled "The Church Missionary Society's Burden: Theological Education for a Self-supporting, Self-governing, and Self-propagating African Anglican Church in Kenya 1844-1930," which was published in the journal *Anglican and Episcopal History* (Vol. 83, No. 1) in 2014. While written by an African scholar, it is an excellent example of Western historiography. It examines the work of the CMS (Church Missionary Society) especially in Mombasa, and the development of a Divinity School begun in 1889 in Freretown. The author has done his research and lists dates and concerns as the Anglican Church in Kenya sought to implement Venn's three-self approach in creating an indigenous church. The CMS sought to create an African educated leadership for this church. Despite a concerted effort over 76 years, by 1920 there were only eight African ordained clergy in all of Kenya (Nkonge 2014:33). Nkonge concludes that much of this had to do with a failure in training indigenous clergy. The point I wish to make, is not the failure of the CMS to create a strong African clergy, but rather to point out that Nkonge's excellent study almost never mentions any African sources of information. His material was all generated by Western missionaries seeking to understand the problem. He is giving us the missionary's answer to the question, not the answer from the people themselves. Why did so few indigenous clergy begin or complete the missionary's programs? If we want to understand this failure in producing African leaders for the Kenyan Anglican Church, we need more than just the missionary's viewpoint; we also need to understand the concerns of the

Africans who were the subjects of this missionary endeavor. This work on the Digo Mission begins to provide that type of historical information.

Another excellent example of a Western history of the CMS mission in Kenya is Steven Paas' *Johannes Rebmann: A Servant of God in Africa before the Rise of Western Colonialism* (2011, VTR Publications). In an early section of this book (pages 14-15) the author discusses "lost material" including German and English manuscripts and letters that have disappeared over time. However he never mentions any African sources in this section or includes any African sources in his bibliography. This is because Western historiography has traditionally undervalued oral tradition and seen it as unreliable. The truth (they believed) was found in written documents and records as well as a systematic approach to analyzing these materials in order to determine the "truth" of what happened. This is problematic, since "truth" is a very uncertain thing, heavily influenced by individual and group biases. As R. Kenneth Kirby notes,

> Historians themselves, for the most part, feel that the thoroughness of their methods enables them to come to some degree of certainty about the truth of the past. Debate persists, of course, and new approaches arise, but when a sufficient number of scholars who share an interest in a certain place and time in history begin to draw similar conclusions about the "what" and "why" of events, and if new evidence continues to support these conclusions, historians may assert that these conclusions are likely true. Criticism of the truth of history often comes largely from outside the discipline, mostly from postmodern thought in linguistics and cultural studies, where relativism and truth is scoffed at. But it is often historians themselves who criticize oral history, claiming that while interviewer bias can perhaps be identified and dealt with, it is harder to peel back the layers of bias that can affect the informant. Thus the same claims of cultural bias that, according to their critics, historians are unable to overcome in interpreting the documents from the past- these same criticisms are leveled by historians at oral history informants. (Kirby 2008: 26-27)

Just because something is written down does not make it any more or less reliable than any other historical source, including oral history. Paul Thompson supports this concept when he writes,

> Social Statistics, in short, no more represent absolute facts than newspaper reports, private letters, or published biographies. Like recorded interview material, they all represent, either from individual standpoints or aggregated, the social perception of facts; and are all in addition subject to social pressures from context in which they are obtained. With these forms of evidence, what we receive is social meaning, and it is this which must be evaluated. (Thompson 1978: 96)

Therefore, we must think about oral history in a different way, as a type of social memory. In the same way that a modern historian must interpret the historical record in the light of everything that happened after the event recorded, so an individual or social group revaluates and interprets events recorded in oral history. As Kirby notes,

> Nevertheless, with the passage of time or with reflection, a person's view of his or her experience will change. Phenomenology, then, actually predicts that oral history informants should change their story with successive retellings; the very telling of the story could cause a reevaluation, so that a retelling the very next day could be different. Phenomenology also tells the historian to look for different perspectives in the view of the informant; in one sentence the informant could be trying to reconstruct his or her perspective at the time of the historical event, and the next sentence could be a present-day evaluation. (Kirby 2008: 30)

It is important that historians not use oral history in the same way they might use traditional historical records. The human memory is simply not designed to retain statistical facts in the same way as the written record. As Kirby (2008: 33) again notes, "When the informant's memory seems vague or unreliable, the interviewer keeps in mind that all of the 'real facts' cannot be known under even the best circumstances and looks rather for truths of understanding, of spirit, of cultural values, that tell the real story of the historical event or era..." It seems most logical to bring traditional historiography alongside of oral history to help present a multilayered understanding of an event. This is especially true in mission history, which records the interaction of two very different cultural groups. Both sides help reveal the truth of a situation, both the factual events and the cultural understanding of the context. After Kirby gives some examples of oral history from his own experience, and thinks about the meaning behind the stories, he notes,

> After all, a factually wrong answer can sometimes tell as much or more about the meaning and values than a technically correct answer. And ultimately the goal of cultural history is not necessarily to arrive at "what really happened" but at what the experience or event, though perhaps misremembered or imprecisely related, means to the informant. (Kirby 2008: 35)

Since most of mission history from the point of view of the missionized is likely to be in the form of oral history and the collective memory, it is vitally important that missiologists learn to utilize oral history effectively to present the most complete history of the local church as possible.

Using Oral History in the Mission History of Digo Land

The reason I am raising this issue started as a simple search. I was determined to at least try and find a first name for Rev. Bans, the mysterious founder of the first Digo Mission in 1904, who left in 1912 after finding the experience too difficult. I consulted several key years of material from the CMS archives on microfilm at Asbury Theological Seminary. The material was full of letters and documents produced by Western missionaries about furloughs, the needs for housing, plans for mission buildings, statistics gathered for reports, squabbles between various missionaries, medical reports, etc. With the single exception of Rev. Wright's report on entering Digo land in 1912, which is reproduced in chapter one, there was no mention of Digo land or a Rev. Bans. I searched page by page, the material from 1904, 1908-1909, and 1911-1913.

Granted, I have not done a thorough complete search of the material, so there is probably much more to be found, but I was struck by the things I didn't find. I found no account of a Rev. Bans, although I did find a Burns, Burt, and Burness who served in Kenya during the correct time period, but none of them fit the description given in the oral history. I also found no account of the burial of the six virgins at Changamwe, or record of Bans' mission being burnt after he left the field. Yet, the CMS archives are one of the most complete and detailed I have seen, and I encountered many documents written by Secretary Binns.

Even more perplexing is the account written by Rev. Wright in 1912, which is reprinted as chapter one of this current volume. This was the year Rev. Bans was supposed to have left the mission field, but no mention is made of him. Rev. Wright and his travelling companions do not report visiting or refreshing themselves at the Zunga mission buildings, which should have still been standing. Despite numerous other historical references, Rev. Wright makes not a single reference to Rev. Bans or his previous eight years of mission work in Digo land. There are references to Muslims, but on the whole they are positive and relations seem to be good. His record of the traditional dances of the Digo people clearly indicate a negative view of the traditional religion, which is not surprising in missionaries from this time. How do we correlate this historical document with the oral history reported by the church elders, and especially recorded in Stephen Gude Zani's unpublished record from 1983 (which I am assuming is based off oral reports as well)?

This is the point where it is important to understand how oral history works, especially as we use it in conjunction with traditional history. Oral history is an ongoing process of communal memory. What is important is not the factual details, but the story itself and the bigger message it aims to communicate. Traditional historical research relies on the historical record, documents or written accounts made close to the time of the original event. Historians cannot use oral history in the same way they use written documents in an archive. The historical record speaks directly to the original context, they are static, unchanging materials which reflect one viewpoint at a particular time and place. Oral history on the other hand is constructed from memory, which is not written down. Therefore it is based on years, often decades, of thinking about the event in the light of changing contexts, and so it is subject to the commentaries made by others in the community as well as changes in the life of the original person who holds the memory. It can change and be added to over time to shape and even change the original meaning. Both types of history are essential for a good understanding of mission history, and both have their strengths and weaknesses.

Conclusion

What have we learned from the study of Digo mission history as related by the elders of the Digo church? Using the ideas outlined by Kirby and discussed above, I believe we have learned four very important things to answer the questions of early CMS missionaries and current Anglican leaders about why the church seemed to fail to grow despite all of the best efforts of the missionaries and the CMS organization.

First, despite their best efforts, the CMS missionaries were never free from the fears and concerns that accompanied them with the British colonial empire. The account of Mwangauchi told by the elders, shows how the fear of British power and the possibility of retaliation was an overriding concern. It does not matter that the British had completely outlawed slavery in the British Empire in 1833; the fear that he might be sold into slavery was a real concern for Mwangauchi and his family even around 1913. That this story is remembered by the community and passed down shows an ongoing communal concern for the outside implications of colonial power. Outsiders, including CMS missionaries, could not be fully trusted. Future Christian mission work will require intense efforts to build trust.

Second, even though there was firm political control by Britain in British East Africa during this time, the story of the virgins at Changamwe demonstrate Christian fears of the Islamic and traditional religious communities. Even if the story is not factually true, the possible rumor of such an event was enough to prevent conversion and probably promote some reconversions back to Islam. Such stories have power, even if they may not be rooted in an actual event. This story coming from the elders in Digo land asserts that such fears are still present and possibly encouraged by Muslim leaders in the area. Building positive bridges with the Muslim community and putting such fears to rest will be an important part of future mission work in Digo land.

Third, the story of Rev. Bans is quite intriguing. Perhaps people have the wrong dates, or the name has changed over time, but more work needs to be done to verify if Rev. Bans was a real historical figure or not. Even if he was not a real person in history, or his name and role has changed in the communal memory over time, I believe he is a composite of how the Digo people viewed CMS missionaries, and perhaps even missionaries today. They come from outside, build their buildings or institutions, and ultimately leave because they cannot handle living in the Digo environment. Missionaries may be good people, with good hearts, but they are ultimately unreliable. Future missions in Digo land will have to be committed to remaining and exhibit an incarnational love for the Digo people that proves a willingness to remain, even in bad situations.

Fourth, the compelling and beautiful accounts of the genealogies of the three Christian families who persevered over time, and have produced some of today's current leaders is a reminder of the strength, commitment, and loyalty of the Digo people. Despite their fear of outsiders, Islamic retaliation, and the unreliable nature of the church leadership, the faithful have continued. This is the story of the oral tradition of the Digo elders.

It is now time for the church to build on this knowledge. Future mission outreach to the Digo needs to come from a place of humility, not power. It needs to preach peace and the presence of God in the face of fear. It needs to be committed to remaining connected to the Digo people- refusing to abandon the people when situations might become difficult. But above all, it needs to invest trust, time, and energy into its relationships with the Digo people, because the church will be rewarded with a strength, loyalty, and commitment that will continue for generations. Above all, the Church must learn to value the oral history of those it has reached for the Gospel. These stories from the elders of the communities can teach us much more than the written records and journals of the missionaries. They can help us understand mission history from a completely different point of view, and teach us how we can learn from our mistakes. This is what World Christianity can learn from the Digo of Kwale County, Kenya.

WORKS CITED

A., Philip Horace R.
>   1936 *A New Day in Kenya*. London: World Dominion in Kenyan Press.

Adelphoi
>   1953 *His Kingdom in Kenya*. London: Hodder and Stoughton.

Anderson, W.B.
>   1981 *The Church in East Africa, 1840-1974*. Nairobi: Uzima Press.

Anderson, K.B.
>   1973 *Religion in East Africa, Book 5*. Nairobi: Evangel Publishing House.

Aldrick, Judith
>   1986 "Leven House," in *Kenya Past and Present*. Vol 18 (1): 43-46 (Accessed October 15, 2018).

Al Mazrui, Shaykh Al-Amin bin
>   1995 *The History of the Mazrui Dynasty of Mombasa*, translated by J. McL. Ritchie. London: Oxford University Press.

Al-Naqira, M. A.
>   1986 *Intisharul Islami fii Sharq Ifriqiya*. Cairo: Darul.

Al-Sayyar, A. A.
>   1975 *Dawlatul-Ya'aribah fii Umman wa Sharq Ifriqiya*. Beirut: Darul-Quds.

Afisi, Oseni Taiwo
    2010 "Power and Womanhood in Africa: An Introductory Evaluation." *Journal of Pan African Studies*, Vol 3 (6):229-238.

Barrett, David
    1982 *The Kenya Churches Handbook: The Development of Kenyan Christianity 1498-1973*. Kisumu: Evangel Publishing.

Barret, Mambo
    1973 *Malauphlin, Kenya Church Handbook The Development of Kenyan Christianity 1498-1973*. Kisumu: Evangel Publishing House.

Baur, John
    1994 *2000 Years of Christianity in Africa: An African History, 62-1992*. Nairobi: Paulines Publications Africa.

Binns, H. K.
    2018 www.thebinnsfamily.org.uk/gedrecord.php?pid=I5264, (Accessed October 16, 2018).

Bolton, Doug
    2016 "Believing in witchcraft can slow economic progress." *The Independent*, May 10, 2016 https://www.independent.co.uk/news/science/witchcraft-economy-africa-a7023081.html (Accessed October 18, 2018).

Chadwick, Henry
    1967 *The Early Church: The Pelican History of the Church*, Volume I. Baltimore: Penguin Books.

Chingamba, Stephen
    2018 Personal Interview, October 22, 2018.

Church, Elisabeth
    1988 *Kenya Under My Skin*. UK: The Paternoster Press.

Conn, H.M.
    1978 "Islam in East Africa: An Overview." *Journal of Islamic Studies* Vol (17), No 2:75-91. Islamabad: Islamic Institute, International Islamic University.

Couplan R.D.
    1938 *East Africa and Invaders, From the Earliest Times to the Death of Seyyid Said in 1856*. Oxford: Clarenndon Press.

Chidongo, Tsawe- Munga
    2012 "Exploring Dialogue: Reflections on Christianity's Mission and African Indigenous Religion." Saarbrücken: LAP LAMBERT Academic Publishing.

    2018 *Shujaa Me Katilili wa Menza: Her Legacy in Independent Africa*. Germany: Lambert Publishers.

Chimera, Rocha
    2018 Personal interview, October 12, 2018.

Chisholm, Hugh, ed.
    1911 "Tarquinius Priscus, Lucius," *Encyclopedia Britannica*, vol 26 (11th ed). Cambridge: Cambridge University Press.

Dawson O.E.C.
    1887 *Bishop James Hannington, First Bishop of Eastern Equatorial Africa, A History of His Life and Work 1847-1885*. London: Seeley and Co.

Dempster, M.A. Klaus, B.D. & Petersen, D.
    1991 *Called and Empowered: Global Mission in Pentecostal Perspective*. Peabody: Hendrickson.

Elspeth, J.
    1972 *Africa: An Early History*. London: George G. Harrap & Co., Limited.

Forum of Bible Agencies International
    2017 "Basic Principles and Procedures for Bible Translation." Retrievedfrom:https://forum-intl.org/resources translation-standards/on January 31, 2020.

Gathogo, Julius
    2008. "The Struggle Against Patriarchalism in Kenya (1980-1992)," *Studia Historiae Ecclesiasticae*, Vol (34), No :265-288.

    2011a "The Challenge of Money and Wealth in Some East African Pentecostal Churches," *Studia Historiae Ecclesiasticae*, Vol (37), No 2:133-151.

    2011b *African Hospitality from a Missiological Perspective*. Saabrucken: Lambert Academic Publishers.

    2013 "History of Ecclesiastical Politics in Kenya," *Online International Journal of Arts and Humanities*, Vol (2), Issue 6:173-181.

    2015 "Ecclesiastical and Political Leaderships in One Armpit: Reconstructing the Memory of Thomas Kalume," *Studia Historiae Ecclesiasticae*, Vol (41), No 3:92-110.

Geoview
    2018 http://ke.geoview.info/godoma,45001848n (Accessed October 21, 2018).

Gore, Lugo
    2018 Personal interview, October 10, 2018.

Harris, Grace Gredys
    1978 *Casting Out Anger Religion Among the Taita of Kenya*. Cambridge Studies in Social Anthropology, 21. London: Cambridge University Press.

Harris Josephy E.
    1977 *Recollections of James Juma Mbotela*. Nairobi: East Africa Publishing House.

Hicks, Andrew
    2010 "Our History." Retreived from: (http://www.lavingtonunited.org/index.php/about-luc/our-history) on January 28, 2020.

Hollenweger, Walter J.
    1972 *The Pentecostals*. London: SCM.

Huskinson, Janet
    2009 "Looking for Culture, Identity and Power." In *Experiencing Rome: Culture, Identity and Power*, edited by Janet Huskinson, pp. 3–28. New York: Routledge.

Holey C.W., C.M.G.
    1929 *Kenya-From Chartered Company to Crown Colony. Thirty Years of Exploration and Administration in British East Africa*. London: H.F. & G Witherby.

Hoyle, Brian
    2000 *Port-City Renewal in Developing Countries: A Study of East African Waterfronts*. Southampton: University of Southampton.

Ibn Battuta, Muhammad Ibn Abdallah
    1987 *Rihlatu Ibn Battuta*. Beirut: Daru Ihyaul-Ulum.

Ingrams, William. H.
    1967 *Zanzibar: It's History and Its People*. London and New York: Routledge.

Jack, Elspeth
    1972 *Africa: An Early History*. London: George G. Harrap & Co., Limited.

Jones, J. D.
    1990 *Poverty and the Human Condition*. Lewston: Edwin Mellen.

Joshuah
    2018   www.africa.upenn.edu/NEH/religion.html (Accessed October 14, 2018).

Judith, A.
    2013 "Leven House," *Sabinet* https://journals.co.za/contentkenya/18/1AJA02578301_599?crawler=true (accessed October 15, 2013).

Juma. M.
    2018 Personal interview, October 10, 2018.

Kesi, Francis
    2018 Personal interview, October 24, 2018.

Kiilu. J.
    2018. Personal Interview, October 10, 2018.

Kisauni
    2018 http://ackkisauniandbinnsschool.com/index.php/brief-history-of-the-church (Accessed October 21, 2018).

Kirby, R. Kenneth
    2008 "Phenomenology and the Problems of Oral History." *The Oral History Review*, 35(1): 22-38.

Krapf, Johann Ludwig
    1860 *Travels, Researches, and Missioanry Labours during an Eighteen Years' Residence in Eastern Africa*. Abingdon, UK: Frank Cass.

Maneno, Johana
    2018. Personal Interview, October 10, 2018.

Maneno, Samuel
    2018 Personal Interview, October 10, 2018.

    2018 Personal interview, October 15, 2018.

Mararo,
>2018 Personal interview, October 21, 2018.

Martin, B. G.
>1974 "Arab Migration to East Africa in Medieval times." *The International Journal of African Historical Studies.* Vol (7), No 3:367-390. Boston University: Boston University African Studies centre.

Matthew, Adam
>1896 *The Church Missionary Atlas.* London: Adams Matthew Digital 2020 and Church Missionary, Societyhttp://www.churchmissionarysociety.amdigital.co.uk/Documents/Details/CMS_OX_Atlas_01.

McGee, Gary
>1994 "Pentecostal Missiology: Moving Beyond Triumphalism to Face the Issues". *Pneuma: The Journal of the Society of Pentecostal Studies,* Vol (16), No 2:208-211.

McClung, L Grant Jr. ed.
>1986 *Azusa Street and Beyond: Pentecostal Missions and Church Growth in the Twentieth Century.* South Plainfield, NJ: Logos.

Middleton, John
>1976 "The Immigrant Communities: The Arabs of the East African Coast," in Low, D. A and Smith, Allison, eds. *History of East Africa,* Vol 3. Oxford: Clarendon Press.

Mlamba, Dorcas Chanya
>2006 "The Woman God Created: Some Cultural Implications for Coastal Bantu People of Kenya." Unpublished PhD Thesis: Auckland University, Australia.

Mugambi, J.
>1995 *From Liberation to Reconstruction.* Nairobi: E. A. E. P.

Munga, Jairus Timeaus
>2018 Personal interview, October 24, 2018.

Munga, Wa-Mumbo
    2018 Personal interview, October 10, 2018.

Mwadama, Isaiah
    2018 Personal interview, October 22, 2018.

Mwakimako, Hassan
    2018 Personal interview, October 12, 2018.

Mwalonya, Shadrack
    2018 Personal interview, October 10, 2018.

Mwangi, Peter
    2018 Personal interview, October 21, 2018.

Mwangudza, J. A.
    1983 *Mijikenda: Kenya's People*. London: Evans Brothers Limited.

Mwatha, Samuel Kang'ethe
    2018 "Pentecostal Surge," *Dictionary of African Christian Theology*, https://dacb.org/stories/kenya/mwatha-samuel/ (Accessed October 25, 2018).

Myers, Bryant
    1999 "Poverty and the poor" in *Walking with the poor*. Maryknoll: Orbis.

Ndara, Patrick
    2018 Personal interview, October 24, 2018.

Ngugi, James
    1964 *Weep Not Child*. Nairobi: Heinmann Education Books.

    1965 *The River Between*. Nairobi: Heinmann.

Nkonge, Dickson K.
    2014 "The Church Missionary Society's Burden: Theological Education for a Self-supporting, Self-governing, and Self-

propagating African Anglican Church in Kenya 1844-1930." *Anglican and Episcopal History*, Vol 83 (1).

Olando, M.
2017 "The State of Christian- Muslim relations in Kenya," https://www.christiantoday.com/article/churches.and.mosques (Accessed October 13, 2018).

Otieno, Jeckonia
2012 "Krapf's Priceless House," *Standard Digital*, https://www.standardmedia.co.ke/business/article/2000062642/krapf-s-priceless-house (accessed 15 October 2018.

Owen, Captain W. F. W.
1833 *Narrative of Voyages to Explore the Shores of Africa, Arabia and Madagascar, Performed in H. M Ships,* Leven *and* Barracouta, 2 vols. London: Bentley.

Paas', Steven.
2011 *Johannes Rebmann: A Servant of God in Africa before the Rise of Western Colonialism*. Tanzania: VTR Publications.

Phiri, I. A.
2000 "Stand Up and Be Counted" in Denise Ackermann, Eliza Getman, Hantie Kotzé, and Judy Tobler (eds.). *Claiming our Footprints: South African Women Reflect on Context, Identity and Spirituality*. Matieland: The EFSA Institute for Theological and Interdisciplinary Research.

Pouwels, R. L.
1978 "The Medieval Foundation of East African Islam." *The International Journal of African Historical Studies*. Vol.11 No. 2. pp 201-226, Boston University: Boston University African Studies Centre.

Pore, Simon Maneno
2018 Personal interview, October 19, 2018.

Ramtu, Elijah Kubeta
2018 Personal interview, October 10, 2018.

Saayman, Willem A.
>1993 "Some reflections on the Development of the Pentecostal Mission Model in South Africa". *Missionalia*, Vol 21, No 1:42-51.

Said, Amira Msellem
>2018 Personal interview at Ahmed Hotel, Old Town, Mombasa, October 3, 2018.

Salim, Ahmed Idha
>1973 *The Swahili-Speaking Peoples of Kenya's Coast 1895-1965*. Nairobi: East African Publishing House.

Samboja, Bryson Kirombo
>2005 "Muslims Use of the Hirizi Charms in Mombasa, Kenya and Their Implications for the Christian Mission." Doctor of Missiology Dissertation, Fuller Theological Seminary, School of Intercultural Studies.

Samboja B. K.
>1996 *The Clearing of Jungles and the Climbing of Hills, the Christian Mission Among the Taita in the Coast Province of Kenya*, Unpublished MA dissertation. Birmingham: Selly Oak Colleges.

Sesi, Stephen Mutuku
>2003 Prayer Among the Digo Muslims of Kenya and its Implications for Christian Witness. Ph.D. thesis for Fuller Theological Seminary, School of World Mission, Pasadena, CA.

Shorter, Aylward and Njiru, Joseph N.
>2001 *New Religious Movements in Africa*. Nairobi: Paulines.

Smith, Warren, S. & Ofundi, Kennedy
>2016 *A Colony of Heaven: Bishop Hannington and Freretown, Early Christian Mission in East Africa*. Parker, Co: Outskirts Press, Inc.

SPA
> 2013 The Kenyan Situation Population Analysis. Nairobi: National Council for Population and Development, http://admin.theiguides.org/Media/Documents/FINALPSAREPORT.pdf (Accessed 18 October 2018).

Sparrow M.
> 2011 *Mission in Mombasa: Ninety Years of Caring for Seafarers at Kilindini*. Nairobi: Missions.

Spear, T.
> 1978 *The Kaya Complex: A History of the Mijikenda Peoples of the Kenya Coast to 1900*. Nairobi: Kenya Literature Bureau.

Stark, Rodney
> 1996 "Why Religious Movements Succeed or Fail: A Revised General Model," *Journal of Contemporary Religion*, Vol 11, No 2: 133–146.

> 1996 *The Rise of Christianity: A Sociologist Reconsiders History*. Princeton, New Jersey. Princeton University Press.

Stenschke, Christoph
> 2009 "Married Women and the Spread of Early Christianity." *Neotestamentica*, 43 (1): 145-194.

Sudarkasa, Niara
> 1986 "The Status of Women" in Indigenous African Societies, *Feminist Studies*, Vol 12, No 1:91-103.

Taabu, Nimrod
> 2018 Personal Interview, October 10, 2018.

Thomas, Spear
> 1978 *The Kaya Complex: A History of the Mijikenda Peoples of the Kenya Coast to 1900*. Nairobi: Kenya Literature Bureau.

Thompson, Paul
>1978 *The Voice of the Past: Oral History*. London: Oxford University Press.

Tinga, K. K.
>2004; 2018 "The Presentation and Interpretation of Ritual rites: The Mijikenda Kaya case." *Journal Museum International*, Vol (56), Issue 3.

Trimingham, J. Spencer
>1980 *The Influence of Islam Upon Africa*. London and New York: Longman Group Limited.

Wandera. J. et al.
>2008 *Christian- Muslim Co-existence in Eastern Africa*, Nairobi: Paulines Publications Africa.

Watt, W.M.
>1944 "The Political Relevance of Islam in East Africa." *Journal of International Affairs*, Vol (42) No 1:35-44.

Welbourn, F. B.
>1965 *Religion and Politics in Uganda*. Nairobi: East African Publishing House.

Zablon, Nthamburi
>1982 *A History of the Methodist Church in Kenya*. Nairobi: Uzima Press.

>1991 *The African Church at the Crossroads, Strategy for Indigenization*. Nairobi: Uzima Press.

Zani, Stephen Gude
>1983 "Mission history in Digo land," unpublished material, July 28, 1983.

www.ingramcontent.com/pod-product-compliance
Lightning Source LLC
Chambersburg PA
CBHW031352040426
42444CB00005B/259